BOOKS BY HARRISON SNOW

*Indoor/Outdoor Team-Building
Games for Trainers*

*Tools for Teams:
The Manager's Guide to Building Teams*

*The Power of Team-Building
Using Ropes Techniques*

# CONFESSIONS
## of a
# CORPORATE
# SHAMAN

## Healing the Organizational Soul

# Harrison Snow

**REGENT PRESS**
Berkeley, California

MANUFACTURED IN THE U.S.A.
Regent Press
Berkeley, California
www.regentpress.net

*To those who strive to be*
*the change they want to see in the world*
*and those who support and encourage them.*

*One sun rose on us today...my face, your face, millions of faces in morning's mirrors...all of us as vital as the one light we move through, the same light on blackboards with lessons for the day...all of us—facing the stars...hope—a new constellation...waiting for us to map it, waiting for us to name it—together.*

Excerpts from "One Today,"
2013 Inaugural poem by Richard Blanco

# Contents

# Overview: What *IS* the Big Idea?

The big idea, like all big ideas, is simple. An organization has its own collective consciousness. That consciousness is the sum of the behaviors, knowledge, beliefs, and values of the individual members, current and past; and it shows up as the organizational culture.

The consciousness of the leadership both influences and is influenced by this collective consciousness, which has an evolutionary impulse to evolve. The forces that push for change inevitably meet internal and external constraints that affect the pace of this evolution. Over time, the culture and its supporting structure will evolve and adapt or be replaced. Motivating staff with a vision of the future and compelling reasons to leave the past behind is helpful but not enough. Change starts with the leaders of change. Leaders need to become the change they want to see in others. By surfacing and addressing their own internal constraints they can identify and address the parallel, and usually hidden, constraints in the collective conscious-ness of their organizations. This book explores the con-nection between the personal consciousness of the change leader with the collective consciousness of the organiza-tion. Use of self, systems thinking, and the knowing field are the three pillars that form and inform this connection. These pillars don't replace the usual change practices, however, which still have their place in corporate offices and off-sites. What the pillars offer is an approach that identifies and resolves the hidden blocks that trap an orga-nization and its leaders in their dysfunctions.

Business leaders sometimes ask me, *"What's new in the field of leadership or organizational development?"* It's embarrassing to admit that most of the practices we use today were developed twenty to thirty or more years ago. That right. It's been that long. One of the first leadership tools, the Myers-Briggs Type Indicator (MBTI) question-naire, was proposed in the 1920s (and is still widely used today).[1] Group change processes like Appreciative Inquiry, popularized by David Cooperrider,[2] a professor of social entrepreneurship, or Open Space Technology, developed by the organizational development consultant Harrison Owen,[3] were introduced in the 1980s. And, as radical as the idea seemed back then, Transcendental Meditation and mindfulness were also offered to the employees of a num-ber of small, forward-thinking companies.[4] One of the most recent of the big ideas, the concept of emotional intelli-gence (EQ) promoted by Daniel Goleman, a psychologist and science writer, debuted in 1995—before the general public had heard of the Internet or could log on.[5]

Every year neuroscience is revealing still more about the astounding potential of the human brain to access knowledge, make connections, and generate new insights. For the first time in recorded history, we can measure how our brains are wired socially. The English poet John Donne seems to have got it right when he wrote in 1624: *"No man is an island,/Entire of itself."* Theories of change increasingly highlight the role of consciousness and neuroscience to explain human behavior. Isn't it time for a new approach that makes use of this vast, untapped potential?

One new approach, which we will explore in this book, is a method called organizational constellations. This method, based on the work of the systemic therapist Bert Hellinger, is just beginning to be recognized in North America as a tool for leadership development and organizational change.

You may be thinking, quite understandably, that what is offered here is too far-out for the cautious and skeptical people you work with. Anything truly new will naturally meet with resistance. If you are a baby boomer you might recall how the practices just described were considered beyond the fringe back in the 1980s. When I first started facilitating team-building and leadership programs at that time, some doubters would look at me askance and say, *"What do you mean teamwork? The boss is going to make all the decisions! Work styles inventory like MBTI are just readings from an astrologer. Emotions have no place in the workplace. And, how could anyone meet without a detailed agenda using Open Space?"* Once people experienced, hands-on, the value of the methodologies listed above, however, the biggest skeptics often morphed into the most ardent fans.

If you are an innovator or an early adaptor who likes to be a few years ahead of the crowd, then this book is written for you. You believe it's time to update our approaches to leadership and change the same way we have been updating our technology and business structures. Yet, anything that is truly innovative will also seem unfamiliar, unpredictable, edgy, or even slightly weird—at least till you've had a few experiences with it. Another decade may pass before organizational constellations becomes a well-known brand for solving challenges, making decisions, enhancing leadership abilities, and managing change. Until then, if you are willing to trade the comfort zone of the known for the discomfort of learning something new, you will enjoy a competitive advantage as a change leader.

# Introduction

Change leaders typically seek to build a culture in which people are aligned around a shared vision, values, and strategy. As part of that alignment, leadership and team skills are developed. Measures, processes, and norms that foster the flow of communication are introduced. Critical problem-solving and decision-making are team based. Risk-taking and innovation are rewarded. Bookcases and websites are crammed with techniques and models that develop the levers of performance listed above. Still, given all we know about building healthy organizations using these standard practices, HR surveys consistently show high levels of dysfunction and discontent in the public and private sectors. The cost of dysfunction in terms of turnover, employee engagement, morale, innovation, and productivity are significant. As these troubles distract our time and attention, globalization continues to scale up competition. The winners are those who are able to contain the office bushfires while, at the same time, learning and innovating faster than the world is changing.

Dysfunction and denial mark the place where learning and adapting are not keeping pace. When a person, team, or organization is afflicted by a learning disability, small issues inevitably grow up to become big, "wicked" ones. People come and go but the dysfunction stays and becomes embedded in the shadows of cultural DNA. Change is difficult because the dysfunction is not in the individual. It is in the collective space between individuals and groups. Standard leadership practices are unaware of these hidden dimensions. Instead of blaming the toxic worker or the ineffective leader, a radically more insightful approach is called for.

The wise change leader faces the global challenges of a flat world with a new mindset, one that inspires access to the subconscious through the emotions, the spirit, and physical sensations. But such a multilateral, systemic approach has disruptive implications. Why? Most corporate professionals are highly educated, and they mastered a rigorous academic curriculum through the mental powers of analysis and conceptualization. Naturally, when solving problems and making decisions, they rely on the same mental domain. Even popular concepts like emotional intelligence (EQ) are presented in a conceptual way that does little to actually develop a leader's emotional skills.[1] Thinking about emotions is easy, yet learning how to manage them, especially in a group setting, demands a skill set outside the conceptual realm. Not surprisingly, many leadership teams regularly fall into "analysis paralysis" or bog down in emotional gridlock. As long as they rely solely on the analytical mind, they access just a portion of their human potential. If we want our organizations to be more functional we have to find a way to go beyond the limitations of the verbal mind. As Einstein said, *"The mind is a good servant but a terrible master."*

Change is driven by insight. These insights emerge when we broaden our spectrum of information. Our visible light spectrum is only a small fraction, *"...less than one-tenth of one percent of what is really there."* [2] As we've learned to take advantage of even small parts of that vast, invisible spectrum, our world has been transformed by such innovations as radio, television, and cell phones.

Like this limited spectrum of light, conceptualization that takes place solely within the limits of the analytical mind excludes a vast range of potential insights. Here is the "gist" of the approach of a corporate shaman. Access more information. Include and transcend the limitations of the mind by making more use of the full spectrum of physical, emotional, psychological, and spiritual intelligences. The shaman in some traditions is the "one who sees." In the corporate world, the aware observer can perceive patterns and implications that others don't. Although I never called myself, or any of my colleagues, a "shaman," facilitators of change have a lot in common whether they work in a conference room or a jungle clearing.

One of these commonalities is the skillful use of your conscious mind in a way that enables you to access the information and insights hidden below the threshold of awareness. Tacit knowledge—what we don't know we know—turns out to be more than we could imagine. If your schooling, like mine, was "mental-centric" then knowledge was exclusively pursued by the intellect. Nonconceptual approaches to understanding were dismissed as "touchy-feely" or "psychobabble." This denigration of the other intelligences is shortsighted. All modalities, subjective and objective, are necessary to fully embrace the challenges and opportunities life offers.

The nonverbal thinking approach is easy to call for but

may seem difficult to do at first. I am sometimes amazed at the white-knuckle grip the verbal intellect has on my colleagues. It feels comfortable and safe to intellectualize and analyze the problems they face. I point out that they can't conceptualize their way to a place of insight and innovation. They have to risk a dip into the "felt-sense" part of their psyches where feelings and sensations lurk just below the surface of awareness. This unarticulated, yet felt within the body, sense of knowing could be a part of ourselves that wants to be heard. Energy from our past is stuck there waiting to be released. Maybe somewhere in our unresolved past there is a small kid who is sad, afraid, or angry. Many expend a lot of energy avoiding or denying those disowned or forgotten feelings, not realizing that this is the path forward for becoming a fully aware person who has the power to lead and innovate.

There are many examples of organizational, social, or even mundane issues where the solutions seem obvious and should work if implemented. Almost all scientists agree that climate change is man-made and will result in serious if not devastating consequences.[3] Likewise, we know that about a third of the population in the United States is obese.[4] The costs of these and other problems are clear. Viable solutions exist. Yet, our unwillingness to act is constrained by factors that can't be grasped by the inner dialogue of the rational, verbal thinking mind.

The Freudian framework offers one explanation for our lack of logical action by assigning the self three parts: ego, superego, and id. The personal ego sets goals. The superego scolds like a parent when those goals are neglected. But the id, the subconscious, ignores them both and imposes what it wants even though the other parts believe they know better. Most people realize from personal experience that our conscious mind can make any number of resolutions. It's our subconscious that determines whether or not our resolutions produce results. In making a decision, the conscious mind has 10 percent of the votes; the subconscious has the other 90 percent.[5] The subconscious is the abode of what we don't know we know; the home of our tacit knowledge. Unless the subconscious considerations are surfaced and addressed, positive change will be a fraction of what is needed.

What is true in one's personal life is also true in the life of an organization. Accessing that reservoir of intelligence enables you or your group to make better decisions and to effectively implement them. This level of intelligence, the knowing field, is accessible to us when our subconscious and conscious minds work together. The roots of our perennial problems, along with their solutions, are hidden in the nonverbal subconscious. If we want deep change, that is where our conscious minds have to look. Currently in the corporate world, the tools used to foster individual or organizational change remain on the level of the conscious, verbal mind. Like the old joke about the drunk doggedly searching for his car keys under the streetlamp, we keep looking there for solutions because that's where the light is. Yet, the essential insights that would rewire the brain for new actions reside in the shadow of the subconscious, beyond the chatter of the inner dialogue.

Accessing these insights requires giving the verbal thinking mind a timeout and focusing attention on the felt-sense of the emotions, the spirit, and physical sensations. Quantum mechanics and neuroscience are often used to explain how vast realms of knowledge can be accessed in a nonlinear fashion that transcends the cause and effect laws of classical physics. The list of relevant articles, books, and blogs about the latest parallels between science and metaphysics grows longer every day. While understanding how nonlinear processes work is important, it's not as crucial as benefiting from them. Few people can explain how a cell phone works, but that does not stop anyone from making a call.

Simplifying complexity and uncovering insights will appeal to those who are divergent, nonlinear thinkers. The Swiss psychologist Carl Jung famously said that the sign of maturity is the ability to hold seemingly opposed ideas together in the mind at the same time. Has your executive team tried the usual approaches yet is still in need of a breakthrough? If so, then utilizing the practices in this book will be worth the perceived risk of doing something unfamiliar.

Change leadership is not an either/or between the objective and the subjective approach. The advanced analytic methods of "big data" highlighted in books such as *Moneyball*,[6] offer effective tools for operational decision-making, especially when the relevant criteria can be measured and expressed numerically. Leadership, however, focuses on the people and the ambiguities that drive individual and group behavior. Because of their inherent ambiguity the most pressing leadership questions cannot be answered numerically. M. Scott Peck understood the dilemma managers increasingly face: *"The more ambiguous our choices the more likely they are to be painful. Inherently, there are no rules for dealing with such ambiguity."*[7]

Collecting and making sense of large datasets take analytical skills. Acting on those data in a meaningful and innovative way, especially when people are involved, demands nonlinear insights. Change leaders who develop their abilities in both domains have an edge over those who discount one over the other.[8]

As the futurist Alvin Toffler predicted, the more high-tech a society becomes the more critical it will be to integrate the hard sciences with high-touch, soft skills.[9] This book explores how to access and use that nonnumerical knowledge to make decisions and solve problems that are people related and systemic. As a leader or consultant, you can draw upon these systemic principles and exercises to breathe new life into how you inspire and conduct change, strategic planning, coaching, leadership development, team-building, and innovation. This mother lode offers a new world of possibilities for those who are willing to use it. To quote Internet marketing guru Seth Godin, *"Our future is created by those who replace the status quo, not those who defend it."*

# PART I

# Losing Your Mind
# and
# Finding Your Senses

*Our educational system, according to some critics, educates creativity out of its students. The emphasis on the "school solution" and getting the right answer trains people to avoid trusting their own inner knowing. The verbal mind has its place, yet any strength overused to the exclusion of other capacities is self-limiting. Developing your nonverbal competencies will deepen your effectiveness as a leader.*

# Chapter 1
# Change Dynamics

**M**achiavelli famously said in the sixteenth century, *"There is nothing more difficult...more perilous to conduct, or more uncertain...than to take the lead in the introduction of a new order of things."* Five hundred years later it has not gotten any easier. The metaphor of turning around an aircraft carrier gives the impression that the leader just turns the wheel and results gradually follow.

Complex systems, however, have complex dynamics that are loaded with unanticipated contradictions and unintended consequences. A ruthless leader might gain compliance—at least in the short term—but gaining the commitment and collaboration that fosters sustainable, long-term change demands a softer set of skills.

Gandhi's admonishment to *"be the change you want to see in the world"* is an essential step that too many leaders neglect with unhappy results. The case study of the Washington, DC, Metro system in chapter 13 ("Wicked Problems") is an example of a long-term attempt to change the culture of a large organization. The soul of the organization may need healing, but until the leadership confronts their own need for inner change, the changes they seek will be stalled. The consciousness of the leader or leadership team affects the collective consciousness of the group. If the leader changes his or her own consciousness, the collective consciousness will change as well. This can work the other way around, too, given their shared connection, but the role of leadership is to take the lead.

This maxim seems simple, obvious, and self-evident. The sticking point is the level of self-awareness and efficacy required. Leaders who are observant and reflective, who seek feedback and address their disowned or never-owned dysfunctions, will have more capacity to change themselves (never an easy task) and then go on to change their organizations. Those who don't have the necessary clarity may use self-deception as a way to defend against overwhelming complexity. If they manage to avoid the temptation to blame others they are still susceptible to the classic dilemma known as the "Abilene Paradox." Leaders and team members can have the best of intentions, yet go along with something they know is suboptimal because they fall prey to the pressures of group think. The outcome of this thinking runs the risk of being a disaster that serves no one.[1]

Another version of this paradox is the learned helplessness that manifests as, "We can't do XYZ because 'they' won't let us." Externalizing your shortcomings lets you off the hook, but it also means abdicating the role of change agent for that of the helpless victim. Looking within is not easy. The blockages to change are often covered by the shadows of the subconscious. There are parts of yourself that are invisible or unknown by you and others. Lateral thinking can't see into those shadows. It takes a multilateral tool like an organizational constellation to bring an invisible dynamic to light so it can be attended to and resolved. Freeing up the energy trapped in a psychological blind spot radically scales up a leader's or even a group's capacity to manage change, especially if the work environment is hyper-complex and opaque. Any enhancement of self-awareness expands one's cognitive bandwidth so there is more capacity to process information and turn it into usable knowledge.

## Soul Field

When we talk about something that is not seen but holds the space for something essential, words like soul, spirit, or field are often used. When we use those words in relationship to an individual or a group, it often has something to do with that person's or that group's essence. The stronger that essence, the more influence it has on the world around it.

Individuals who identify with each other create their own collective field of influence. This group soul or field, in turn, influences the conscious and unconscious behaviors of the individual members.

Much of that influence is shaped by events and people in the past as well as the present. Joining the Boy Scouts or becoming a member of an outlaw motorcycle gang could, over time, dramatically affect your character and actions in drastically different directions.

In 1894 the French sociologist Emile Durkheim introduced the concept of collective consciousness to explain aspects of group behavior. This concept also tells us something about organizational behavior. According to Durkheim, *"The totality of beliefs and sentiments common to the average members of a society forms a determinate system with a life of its own."*[2] This force operates stealth-like under the radar of awareness. Bringing it to awareness enables more choice over how its influence will affect you.

Developing mission statements and their supporting values and norms is one of the standard outcomes of a corporate retreat. Their purpose is to foster positive behaviors. Yet, they seldom change how people interact with each other. The unwritten culture, how people actually behave, is determined by the collective consciousness the members cocreated over time. The different parts of our own personal self all come together in a collective yet unseen whole we call the soul. An organization is similar in that the different parts form a collective gestalt that we could call its soul field. Symptoms of dysfunction emerge when the connections within this field are disrupted.

Oscar Miro-Quesada, a Peruvian shaman and psychologist, captures the essence of the corporate shaman approach in his description of working with *"...seen and unseen worlds with the intention to heal and restore harmony among people, social institutions and nature."*[3] Restoring harmony is the work of the corporate shaman when those institutions are corporations or agencies made of groups that reside in their own self-made world. Many of the components affecting this harmony are hidden below the level of awareness. The shaman accesses those hidden components and helps restore the broken connections that hinder the flow of information between them.

## Going Beyond 3D

Not being able to see something does not mean it does not exist. Dark energy and dark matter are invisible to us but they hold our universe together. The soul of a group may not have a material substance, but you can still feel it and see its effect on others. The wise leader will notice and work with that influence instead of ignoring it.

When a group starts to open up on more than the

mental level, something happens that is hard to put into words. Something new and different emerges and touches the people in the room. A change takes place in you, and consequently and inevitably a change takes place in others who are part of your world. If reality is cocreated, then when your part of that cocreation is altered, the whole picture shifts. As stated in the beginning of this book, tacit knowledge is what you don't know you know. If you can access that knowledge, insights become available that lead to new possibilities. Tacit knowledge resides in a field of intelligence below the threshold of awareness. Since all individual consciousness is connected at the subconscious level this knowledge resides in the collective unconsciousness of the group. The collective unconsciousness has also been described as interchangeable with or representative of the zero point field, the morphogenetic field, the unified field, and the big mind, or the knowing field. In this book we will call this place of knowledge and intelligence the knowing field.

It won't serve our purpose here to attempt to explain how these fields work or even to try to prove they exist. Even Einstein attempted to explain the unified field but did not succeed.

Perhaps that is why he once said, *"There comes a time when the mind takes a higher plane of knowledge but can never prove how it got there."*

Like Einstein, let's not worry about proving anything. If unexpected, but often profound, insights arise in that higher plane then that is good enough. The foundations for accessing this knowing field include the following domains:

❏ *Multimodal:* Mental, spiritual, physical, emotional, and psychological
❏ *Multidimensional:* Conscious, subconscious, and collective consciousness

❏ *Phenomenological:* Working with "what is" in the physical world instead of theories or expectations of what should be

One metaphor to help you visualize this knowing field is to see the approximately three pounds of gray matter in your head as your computer. Bring online your heart and gut, which also contain millions of neurons, and you create a supercomputer. Establish your online connection to other supercomputers through an invisible field of knowing and you've entered the realm of quantum computing. Three pillars that help us utilize this amazing realm are:

❏ *Use of Self:* Gaining insight into an organizational system by noticing how and where its issues resonate within your own personal system
❏ *Systems Thinking:* Observing the organization or group, the relationships between their component parts, and the systemic patterns that may arise
❏ *The Knowing Field:* The field that connects each individual subconscious; it is a reservoir of tacit knowledge, accessed through methodologies based upon the foundational worldviews mentioned above

So, how do we draw upon these foundations and utilize the pillars in a way that can be operationalized to produce insights and inspire change? An organizational constellation is a highly versatile tool that enables leaders to make sense of situations that challenge them with their complexity and opaqueness. In addition to leadership development and change management, this tool can be applied to many different situations leaders face. Case studies that illustrate a number of those situations are detailed in this book. And, even though those case studies will walk you through the sequence of steps followed by the facilitator, it's important for you to appreciate the three pillars—and the worldview they represent—that are behind those steps.

As the facilitator or leader you can't take anyone to a place you have not gone to yourself. Any blind spot or lack of self-awareness limits your capacity in that area. The skillful use of self utilizes the knowledge that arises from the observation of yourself in relationships with others. In effect, you stay one step ahead of your client or group using the space provided by that step to facilitate what needs to unfold.

Systems thinking helps you see what should happen and what is in the way in that space. The process breaks a challenge or issue into its component parts and the desired outcome. Identifying those parts and physically mapping their relationship to each other illustrates the nature of the breakdown and where it occurred.

The knowing field is accessed through the use of representatives who stand in for key parts of the system. The interactions between the representatives uncover the insights and actions that lead to the desired outcome or solution.

In traditional societies, the shaman uses symbols and ritual to create a sacred space. In this space, he or she has access to a heightened state of awareness. According to Malidoma Patrice Somé, "...we enter into ritual in order to respond to the call of the soul."[4]

Somé also says, "What goes wrong in the visible world is only the tip of the iceberg. So to correct a dysfunctional state of affairs effectively, one must first locate its hidden area, its symbolic dimension, work with it first and then assist in the restoration of the physical (visible) extension of it..."[5]

Both the shaman and the facilitator/leader are in service to others. Their ability to help others come to terms with the dysfunctions in their system depends, however, on the extent to which they have done the same with themselves. Whether it is through a vision quest or 360-degree feedback, some form of self-knowledge—through self-observation and reflection—is called for.

You may recall the motto on President Harry Truman's desk: *"The buck stops here."* The motto is fine for those who react to change but insufficient for those who will be the change they want in the world. "The buck *starts* here" is the motto for the holistic leader or facilitator who seeks to drive change. An experience I had when I was first introduced to the systemic approach demonstrates the central role the use of self plays.

## Wherever You Go, There You Are

The first time I facilitated a constellation was at a training seminar in Holland. About a hundred people in the organizational development field came from around the world to a charming village outside Amsterdam. In my learning group we set up current business challenges using the constellation process. I had recently started working with a client on a change initiative. I was wondering if my assessment of the dynamics within the client system was on track. Even though the project was in the beginning stages, I felt I should have more engagement or traction. Was patience the answer or was there something else? Representatives for the leader and her three direct reports were selected and placed as indicated in Figure 1-1.

I stood outside the system and just observed. With her hands on her hips, the first manager communicated she was in charge. Was there any resentment about her style? Two of the other managers seemed to be aligned with her and accepting of her dominance. As the representatives noted their feelings and impulses toward each other, something

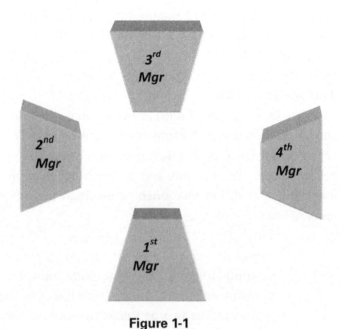

**Figure 1-1**

seemed familiar to me, but unnamable. What could that be? I asked myself. Without dwelling on the question I decided to enter the system and notice what might change. The representative for the leader took a hard look at me and declared authoritatively, *"We don't want you here."*

Her tone took me back a step. Again, the message felt physically and emotionally familiar. Not only had I set up my client system, I had set up my own family system. The first manager was my older sister. The second manager, who was in a power struggle with the leader, was me. The third and fourth managers were my younger siblings who sided with my older sister. It was no accident I was working with this system. But was the client system actually as dysfunctional and triangulated as my family or was it just my projection? Before I could interact objectively with my actual clients, I realized, I had some family history to deal with. A door swung open that I did not know existed. The

good news was that as I changed the inner fundamentals
of my family relationships, the depth of my consulting work
also would change.

## The Mapping Key

The tapered side of each of the symbols in Figure 1-1
shows the direction each representative faced based on my
sense of how they were relating to each other. The proto-
cols below are used in this and all the other diagrams in
this book to map the relationships between the different
parts of the system:

- People, as individuals or groups, are represented
  by a quadrilateral. The short side indicates the
  direction in which the representative is facing.
- A concept, like an organizational vision, is mapped
  with a square or oval.
- Representatives of people, things, or concepts
  are italicized.
- When a person is representing him- or herself in
  the constellation case study, his or her name is
  not italicized.
- Normal script is used to indicate the actual
  issue holder when he or she participates in the
  constellation.
- The quadrilateral that is highlighted represents
  the issue holder.
- Fictional names are used and circumstances
  have been modified to protect anonymity.

## Chapter 2
# First Pillar: Use of Self

U se of self as a model for change has two parts: the group and yourself. The place to start is with the group you lead as a manager or facilitator. An organizational system that needs your help has three subparts or components: the group, the issue, and the source of the issue. The group could be the organization you lead or the client you support or the people you work with. Figure 2-1 is a simple digram to show these three components.

As a leader or consultant you are always alert for issues that need to be addressed. Any issue is really a symptom. You know symptoms are not the problem. The cause is the problem. Low morale, poor productivity, declining

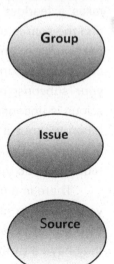

**Figure 2-1**

revenues, questionable quality, staff turnover, or disrespectful workplace behaviors are all symptoms. They have a cause, which needs to be identified and addressed. Knowing this, you conduct interviews, run surveys, and review data that might reveal the contributing factors behind the symptoms. Some consulting is straightforward. The cause is right there. It just takes the fresh eyes or the "beginner's mind" of an outsider to see it. Other causes are not so visible. The ambiguity and smoke of the past test your diagnostic skills. Seeing through the haze depends upon the clarity of the "self" you bring to the task.

The old saying that "You teach what you most need to learn" also applies. Figure 2-2 shows this second part of the model.

No matter where you go, there you are—along with your personal baggage and insecurities. Your issues show up as charged feelings and overreactions. It takes a fearless look within oneself to find the source of those issues. Some of the source might be in your conscious awareness. More often it is hidden in your subconscious. Since the subconscious is unconscious, finding any resolution without a tool like constellations is daunting. Courage and curiousity are required to do your inner work.

**Figure 2-2**

There is a natural resonance between your issue and your team's or client's issue. That resonance is one reason you are both drawn to work with each other. Clients know they have a problem and just want your help with finding the solution. Long explanations about the theories and tools you use won't hold their interest. If you have confronted your own similar issue and have consciously addressed its source in a constructive manner, then odds are you won't get in your own way or the client's. If you have not, then your ability to help or lead will be less than optimal.

In Figure 2-3 you can see how the two parts of the use of self as a model come together.

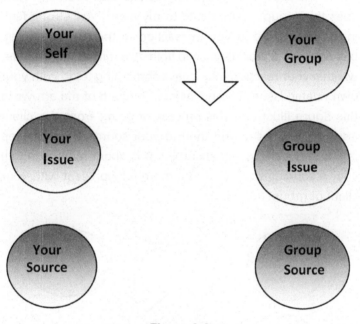

**Figure 2-3**

In situations where the group is your client, you may not know in advance what their issue is and how your own is related to it. Just being alert to this possibility supports the process of finding out. The first step of an engagement is to connect with the group, as is shown in the bent arrow in the illustration above. You learn about them as individuals and as an organization. What do you observe in their interactions? Do you notice certain patterns of behavior? How the client group treats you is typical of the way they treat each other. There is no reason to take any of this personally because it is just data. In Figure 2-4 the top four circles are mostly at the level of conscious awareness. What is hidden in the subconscious is at the source level. At that same source level is the solution or the insight as well. Change is problematic unless you consider the subconscious realm where the potential for change resides. Ask yourself, "How does this group's issue relate to my own?" Are strong feelings bubbling up in you in reaction to the way the group behaves? If so, then it's wise to hold up a mirror and consider whether your reaction might have something to do with your own related issues and behaviors. The path of the arrows in this figure illustrates this process of going from the client issue to your issue and then to your source. This side step is not about being self-absorbed. It is about marshaling all your resources so you can be more fully present with your client or group.

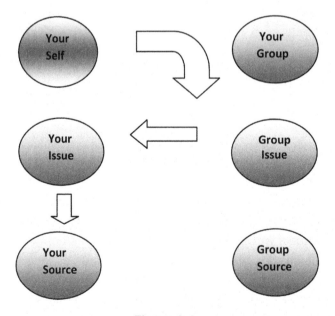

**Figure 2-4**

Even if you believe the precept behavior is data, you might still notice that certain behaviors toward you or toward others triggers reactions within you. Instead of ignoring or denying those reactions or passing judgment on what you observe, try making the connection back to some disowned part of yourself. That part could resemble what you are judging in the group. Taking responsibility also will take you to your resourceful self. Start by noticing *"what is"* in the present moment without the impulse to lecture, defend, fix, or avoid. Working with a sense of calm objectivity and acceptance gives space for your genius to emerge (Figure 2-5).

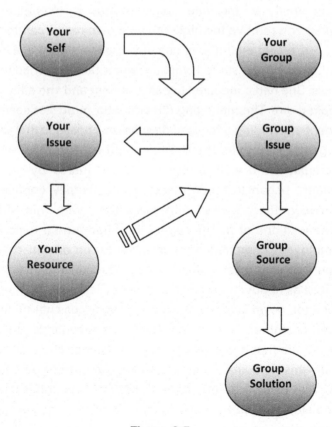

**Figure 2-5**

Once we can see clearly *"what is"* from a resource-ful state, then questions such as *"What is needed in this moment?"* will help reveal the relevant answers.

Overcoming your group's resistances and defenses is a lot easier if you first overcome your own. Before you intervene with the group, especially one prone to express-ing intense emotions, you may need to intervene with yourself. The biggest obstacle to your own resourcefulness is the belief that others are putting you in a non-resourceful state. In actuality, they are handing you a gift that enhances how you show up in the world. Once you find the resolu-tion you need, you can guide others to find what they need. Your ability to facilitate breakthroughs is strengthened when you remove the blocks to your own resourcefulness.

A recent example of use of self played out for a con-sultant who had started working with a family-owned busi-ness. She had conducted her assessment and the situation looked dire. The managing director who hired her seemed adept at avoiding a focused discussion on issues that were urgent and sizable. The business had been started by his parents. It did well until competition, fueled by global-ization, began to erode market share. Family conflicts— between the parents, with the father, with his sister, who was one of the managers too—had turned toxic. The employees complained relentlessly but no one in charge could or would listen and respond. The consultant was at a loss as to how to proceed since her client, the managing director, never seemed to have time to discuss her findings and recommendations. As I heard the consultant's story, it struck me that it might not be just by chance she ended up with this particular client. I asked her about her own fam-ily. She paused in thought and then confessed her family had similar dysfunctions: siblings who were not talking to each other; parents and grown children who were at odds because of past hurts. I suggested that if she found a way to reopen communication and find reconciliation with her own family it was more likely she could do the same for her client. The first step was coming to terms with her own painful past. Once she shifted, then she would help her client shift into a space of more peace and possibilities.

## The Model

The use of self model described above came out of my own phenomenological experiences. I've worked with hundreds of teams since 1988; some of the engagements lasted several years, but most were a few weeks or months long. Looking back I wonder why it took so long for me to see this use of self. It might not have been noticeable to others, but it was noticeable to me that my insecurities, hiding comfortably in the shadow of the subconscious, habitually showed up in certain group settings. I kept reliving the same reality until I took responsibility for and addressed those insecurities. Taking responsibility enables "your ability to respond." Letting go of perfectionism and acknowledging the limits of one's ability is the essence of an empowered humility. Shortcomings, like stray cats, are bound to show up, so it's best to treat those parts of one's own self with compassion. Your sense of purpose may come from the early, often difficult, experiences that shaped who you are. According to the myth of the hero's journey, your wounds determine your gifts.[1]

Not so long ago I was working with an organization that seemed hyper-dysfunctional. They were in the middle of planning and launching a national program that was focused on improving public health in a critical area. The manager was capable and smart but had numerous constraints to deal with. It did not seem they could, as a group, get anything done. The night before our retreat I checked into the conference center after a long drive. I must have given the desk clerk the impression I could not do anything right either. Scattered and disorganized, I rummaged around for my passport and credit card and then went through the same routine again as I tried to exchange some dollars for the local currency.

Reviewing the agenda that night I wondered how anything productive could come of the meeting if both the facilitator and the group were gripped by this scattered incompetence. Failure seemed inevitable. Were these dark feelings and thoughts connected to something in my past? I remembered years earlier, as a new lieutenant in the military, how overwhelmed and underprepared I felt. As a novice leader I made plenty of mistakes, eventually gaining the confidence and leadership skills needed to be effective. In my own family I was sure my father and grandfathers had similar moments of self-doubt and setbacks. Even though they were all deceased, silently I asked for their blessings.

Thinking about the people who would be attending the retreat, clearly I was no better or worse than them. We were all in this together and if we shared a problem we also shared the solution. As I went through these inner acknowledgments and movements, the nagging "sense of gloom caused by an impending sense of doom" started to ease. My mood lightened and a restful night followed. The next morning I felt ready to face a hundred or so disorganized participants.

Surprisingly, instead of chaos the group exhibited a fair degree of coherence and order. During our discussions and activities, themes emerged that were positive and solution focused. Reconnecting with my own sense of competence seemed to hold the space for the group to reconnect with theirs. This parallel process of working with your client by working first with yourself suggests a subtle link between personal and group effectiveness. To be effective at the organizational level, it is best to stay one step ahead on the personal level. Rapid results by the group depend to some extent on rapid learning through self-inquiry by the facilitator or leader.

## Emotional Hijacking and the Self

All of us have had one of these moments. A certain person says something or acts in a particular way and it triggers a strong reaction in you. When one of your "hot buttons" gets pushed you have less access to your emotional and intellectual resources. You've "lost your wisdom" as people say in the Middle East. Physiologically, the frontal cortex has shut down and the amygdala—the abode of fight, flight, or freeze in the limbic system—takes over. When we're in physical danger, the hijacking by the amygdala might be appropriate and even life-saving. But in most social or business situations, losing one's composure means doing or saying things that cause regret. To respond optimally you need to access all your inner resources. A popular saying in the therapeutic professions is that a person is never upset for the reason she thinks she is. For the use of self to work, it is essential that you know your emotional hot buttons and how to manage them. Letting a hot button dictate your reaction when you are facilitating or leading others can't help but lead to a regrettable outcome. If you can calm yourself during a stressful situation then you can calm and reassure others. The part within that needs calming is often wounded or insecure. The more intense its reaction to a situation, the bigger the trauma that is behind the reaction. Knowing the situations or behaviors that trigger those parts of yourself will help you deal with them.

Byron Katie is a facilitator who focuses on personal change by helping people question their habitual thoughts and beliefs. Her method, referred to simply as "*The Work*," offers a way to stay centered while dealing with adversity.[2] Strong emotions often spring from hasty judgments about another person's behavior. Those judgments are based on assumptions about what the offending behavior means that are rooted in a past experience. If you decide that the story you tell yourself about those assumptions is not true and you drop it, what changes for you? What shifts when you stop arguing with reality and "agree to what is"?

## Agree to What Is

There are two parts to "agreeing to what is." The first is forming a clear picture of the reality being addressed. Acknowledging objectively "what is," no matter how we are reacting to it, subjectively provides us with inner space to take the next step. That second step is about not resisting or arguing with reality. People often go through a process of denial, anger, bargaining, and grief before they can come to terms with something they find unacceptable. Elisabeth Kübler-Ross wrote extensively on this emotional sequence as it related to the stages of grief.[3] Unlike the passivity of being resigned, these two inner steps are strengthening. More inner resources are freed up and available to deal with the challenges you face.

## Maintaining Your Objectivity

Many consultants believe their effectiveness depends on being careful not to merge with the client system. An outsider sees things an insider might miss or be reluctant to point out. A healthy separation allows you, the observer, to observe in an objective manner. The client's issues and dysfunctions may seem unrelated, but if you look deeply enough into your own psyche or family history you may find places of resonance and relatedness. Blindly projecting your own issues and insecurities onto your client's is more likely to occur when your subjectivity is not managed properly. Noticing when tendencies are triggered, but not being swayed by them, is the skillful use of self.

Putting space between you and your reactive parts that judge or withdraw enables you to use them as data. Viewing these data as part of your organizational assessment depersonalizes the situation and defuses the potential for a damaging conflict. If we don't resist, collapse, or counterattack then we can inquire and use what we learn in a professional manner.

## Waiting for Enlightenment

How you respond to difficult circumstances and challenging personalities is the litmus test for leadership. That said, you don't have to wait for enlightenment to be an effective leader or facilitator. Overcoming the mind-based defenses against self-awareness enables you to lead others through their denials and blind spots. Brain researchers like Daniel Siegel, professor of clinical psychiatry at the UCLA School of Medicine, are discovering how neuropathways formed in childhood dictate patterns of perception and response that are not based in present time.[4]

The human brain is malleable and, according to Siegel, keeps developing even after childhood. He argues that the mind is not an output of the brain alone; it matters, but so do our social relationships and experiences. *"The mind is embodied not just enskulled."*[5] A mind hardwired to produce a dysfunctional, reactionary pattern can replace that pattern with one that is more functional. Observing your emotions, assumptions, and beliefs and challenging them disrupts those automatic reactions. The hard part is having enough self-witnessing to question the meaning your mind automatically assigns to events. Transcending the neurological and mental grip of the past activates a higher level of cognition. Siegel calls this level of cognition "mindful awareness." You perceive in the moment without the distortions of judgments and interpretations.

According to Siegel, the state of mindful awareness supports the attributes of curiosity, openness, acceptance, and love. The small mind, with its fearful survival-mode reactions, is replaced by a consciousness that is connected to a more universal intelligence and knowing.[6]

How do you replace the biased interpretations of your reactionary mind with mindful awareness? The explanations the mind excels at will inevitably get in the way. Meditation, mindfulness exercises, journaling, personal coaching, and the practices and methods described in this book are some of the means that develop mindful awareness. Constellations bypass the mind's defenses and reveal the hidden emotions and beliefs underlying its bias. Observing yourself rewires the neural pathways that support functional behavior. This awareness is like keeping a window open on your personal computer that is not running any applications. You see from that place what is going on without becoming identified with it. That inner space enables more freedom of choice.

Neither the other-focused nor the self-centered person has a healthy sense of self. Both types are compensating in dysfunctional ways for the parts of the self that were traumatized during their formative years. Fortunately, the opportunity for self-renewal comes with the effort to be self-aware.

### Strengthening Your Sense of Self

Psychotherapist Virginia Satir developed some of the basic concepts for family systems therapy. One of Satir's principles is, *"We must not allow other people's limited perceptions to define us."* [7] Until we define and affirm our own core self, we may tend to be overly influenced by others, vainly trying to please everyone but ourselves. Lord Tennyson, the poet laureate of Great Britain and Ireland during Queen Victoria's reign, described in a letter how he tapped into his creative spirit by affirming his sense of self. *"This (state) has often come upon me through repeating my own name to myself silently, till, all at once out of the intensity and conscious of the individuality, the individuality itself seems to dissolve and fade away into boundless being..."* [8]

Tennyson was on to something that relates to the concept of "kenosis," a word from ancient Greece used by early Christians to connote the emptying of the self. A more modern phrasing is to "get out of your own way."

Getting out of your own way occurs when you let go of the hyper-mental state called being too self-consciousness. This inner movement enables you to respond to the needs of the moment with an emergent knowing. Paradoxically, this getting your "finite self" out of the way starts with a healthy sense of one's individual existence. Vedic masters, like Sri Ramana Maharshi, believed focusing on the felt-sense of "I am" was the gateway from individual to universal awareness. Whether or not you are a poet, a mystic, or a business leader, it is empowering to strengthen the internal sense of your own being. Personal empowerment requires a self to empower. The following exercise for self-strengthening comes from a workshop conducted by family therapist Skip Ellis.[9]

*Place a hand on your chest. Close your eyes and take a few deep breaths. Go within and find the felt-sense of your essence, however you experience it. Think or say quietly from that place deep within yourself:*

❏ *I am*
❏ *I exist—I exist for my own sake*

*You can add lines like the following:*

❏ *I am enough—I am worthy —I matter —I have a place*
❏ *I feel good about myself in the presence of others*
❏ *I am in charge of my life*

Smile to yourself and feel the essential essence of being you. Don't worry if this exercise brings up some difficult feelings. Breaking the habit of looking to others for self-referral or validation might not be comfortable. It can take practice to locate that good feeling of being you just for yourself without relying on anyone or anything else. A resilient sense of self is the inner foundation to stand on when interacting with a challenging person or group. It is your home base when events threaten to throw you off balance.

A strong emotional reaction can cause you to lose your sense of self in the present moment. A simple practice of somatically checking in with your "self-essence" during the day strengthens your gravitas and "groundedness." A healthy sense of self is the summation of who you are and what you stand for. It lies underneath the constant mind stream of random thoughts. This felt-sense is the mindfulness that gives you the wherewithal to resist peer pressure and "speak truth to power." (This phrase is related to civil disobedience that may have come from the Quakers or the African-American community.) Even when interacting with strong personalities, you can stay connected to who you are and what you believe. This exercise is especially helpful for those who tend to focus all their energies externally on others. Saving some of that energy to focus on your inner self enables you to hold on to you while still extending yourself to others.

## I and Thou

A favorite book of mine is *I and Thou* by the Jewish mystic Martin Buber.[10] Buber's theme is that a relationship can be one of engagement and presence—that is, I and Thou—or one of objectification for utilization or gratification—I and It. Obviously the former requires more from us spiritually, psychologically, and emotionally. The more we bring to our "meeting" with the "other," truly seeing and relating, the more there is the fullness of an authentic relationship. A networking event where people shake hands while looking around for someone who is a better contact typifies an I and It relationship. The opposite of that distracted handshake is an intimate, often unexpected, moment where you truly see the other and in turn are seen. A chance meeting with a stranger on a bus or chatting with a family member while washing the dishes may unexpectedly offer the nurturing space of I and Thou.

Something Buber does not dwell on, however, is the tendency of some to indiscriminately and unconsciously relate to others in the mode of I and Thou. The term "unskilled empath," coined by Rose Rosetree, a workshop leader and author, describes this trait.[11] If you are an unskilled empath, too often you lose your sense of self as you listen attentively to the unrestrained chatter of another. Afterward you feel tired and burdened with emotions that are not your own. Rose suggests one antidote is to consciously and selectively relate from the perspective of I and It. The habitual I and Thou relater is not obligated to always feel what others are feeling. Adjusting this inner relating from a "Thou" to an "It" enables the empathic person to consciously maintain the energetic boundaries that define a healthy sense of self.

Other subtle aspects affect the quality of how we relate to each other. According to Thomas Hübl, a German mystic who resides in Israel, we are so busy with our own internal stories we cannot see with fresh eyes the people in front of us. Their essence is revealed when we let go of our preconceptions based on the past. Intimacy happens in moments that transcend time or past experience. If we view life like a professional moviemaker views a movie, according to Hübl, we sense the backstory that underlies each scene. A part of us becomes the observer who does not get lost in the drama being acted out.[12] That space of the observer is where the use of self and the knowing field intersect.

### I Have a Job?

Not too long ago I was talking to a longtime friend on the phone. She mentioned that a mutual acquaintance of ours was struggling. "You are doing better," she told me, "because you have a good job." Her declaration took me back. I have a job? I thought. "It's not really about the job," I replied to my friend. "Jobs come and go. What I have is a mission."

When I got out of graduate school, I spent a year looking for a job during a recession. It was embarrassing. Every time I met someone the first question I was asked was, "What do you do?" or "Where do you work?" Not having a ready answer my self-identify—and my self-esteem along with it—took many hits during my protracted job search. At some point I decided that who I was could not be dependent on the job I held. Why tie my sense of self to something that was bound to change? Ironically, when I finally joined a company, the question "What do you do?" no longer came up so frequently. Later, when I started my own firm, that unconditional sense of myself provided a grounded place to stand on that helped draw in clients. My sense of self gained more gravitas when I defined my mission. During a workshop with a group called the Mankind Project, I realized my mission was to foster a peaceful and productive world by facilitating change and transformation.[13] This realization was the compass I would use to follow my passion. Whether a group loved how I worked with them or not, at least I knew I was doing my mission.

Mark Twain aptly put it this way: *"The two most important days of your life are the day you are born and the day you find out why."* Knowing your mission has two components: the specific and the general. An elderly lady I knew, Thelma Clark, was well regarded at the church I attended. She had gone through a lot growing up as an African-American in the segregated South and would share her wisdom with those in need. One young man called and confided nearly in tears that he had just lost his job. Thelma's reply stayed with me and I am sure with that young man. *"What do you mean you lost your job?"* she retorted. *"Your only job is to grow."*

## The Use of Self and Self-awareness

We all have a self that we can't help but use no matter what role we take on in the workplace. The question to ask yourself is this: "How skillfully am I using my 'self'?" The parts of us that limit our effectiveness are usually hidden from us. It's those aspects of our own self we don't know about or deny in some way that are most likely to trip us up. We tend to see ourselves as we would like to be. The phenomenon of favorable self-deception is called the self-serving bias or the Lake Woebegone effect, in that all the children are considered above average.

Skillful leaders are self-aware. They learn from their experiences. They know that denial or overconfidence blocks the ability to learn. Self-awareness comes from self-observation. The quiet, nonverbal part of the mind is the home of your inner observer. This is where you let go of ideologies and preconceptions about what should be. From this quiet place you can see "what is" and respond intelligently. Meditation strengthens this inner observer that silently notices what is going on with the rest of you. Instead of mindlessly acting and reacting, self-observation enables you to stop, reflect, and choose the optimal way forward. Be your own detective. Notice patterns or overreactions you typically have with others. Give each of those patterns or reactions a name. Explore the underlying causes. Working with them in this manner will free you from their grip. As you learn how to gain insights to foster your own transformation, you will be better able to help others do the same. The verbal thinking mind fills up the space between the ears with chatter about the past or the future. Creativity starts when you break this endless inner loop of recycled, often negative, thoughts. The science fiction writer Ray Bradbury gave similar advice. *"Don't think. Thinking is the enemy of creativity. It's self-conscious and anything self-conscious is lousy."*

One way to strengthen the inner observer is through the simple activity of walking. Whenever you go for a walk outdoors, even if it is only for a city block or two, ask your verbal mind to take a short break. Notice your surroundings with just your nonverbal mind. When your verbal mind interjects, usually with recycled chatter about the past or the future, come back to the quiet now of the nonverbal mind. This practice frees up your brainpower to respond intelligently to the present moment. If this brainpower, like the RAM of a computer, is mostly busy rehashing the past or worrying about the future, it will lack the resources to focus effectively on what life offers in the now.

## More Use of Self

The systemic use of self requires that you put some inner space between you, the observer, and you, the doer. Observing the group as a leader or a facilitator is part of your job. Getting yourself out of the way so you see with objective clarity requires a degree of self-confrontation. Everything that happens becomes a data point that informs your assessment of what else needs to happen. The following case study provides insight into how the "self" can be used as a change management tool.

Ron was asked to facilitate an office retreat off-site. It was supposed to be a straightforward one-day event. The organization was looking to move from one-off projects to conducting capacity building at the national or transnational level. The purpose of the retreat was to discuss this significant change in mission and the strategy needed to achieve it.

The leader for this group seemed unusually nervous that the retreat would devolve into a free for all of complaints and accusations. His concern, while extreme, was not unfounded. Morale was low and frustrations high, given the uncertainty people were experiencing. Ron tried to assure the manager that discontent would not morph into rabid rebellion. A better decision is reached when people can disagree openly with each other and their leader in a professional manner.

The leader seemed mollified at first, but he continued to voice his criticism and displeasure as the date for the retreat drew closer. These expressions were easier for Ron to take when he reflected that he only had to deal with the manager for a few weeks. The staff, however, faced their manager's moods every day. He was treating Ron like he treated others, so from a data collection perspective there was no reason to take this personally. He was demanding a guarantee of safety, yet a sense of safety is ultimately an inside job. His hypervigilance ironically made people feel less secure. The day before the retreat the manager demanded that Ron not allow any "wallowing" by staff in self-pity or blame. Ron countered that if people were forced to be relentlessly positive they would be convinced that the retreat was a failure. The manager nodded but did not look convinced.

Ron left the meeting feeling uneasy. Would the manager ask people to be frank and then chastise the first person who spoke up? Would he let others give voice to their views or would he impose his own version of reality? If it were the latter, the retreat would be long, dull, and unproductive.

Taking responsibility for his part, Ron asked himself where he might have sent mixed messages during the planning meetings, putting one foot on the gas and the other on the brakes. He was not the uber-leader type who could not tolerate dissent, right? A lengthy conversation with his wife followed. She pointed out how he also acted in ways that were driven by fear. Ron realized he had his own inner tyrant that could come down hard on others. Wholeness comes from embracing each and every part of oneself. As Ron connected with his own hypervigilant self, something relaxed within. The sense of resistance he felt toward the manager faded. If he represented some aspect of Ron's self, then who or what was there to resist or resent? He could appreciate the perspective that it made no sense to discuss how people felt about difficult issues that were a fait accompli. No matter how the manager showed up Ron felt ready to respond with clarity and compassion.

The next morning the staff arrived at the conference center in a relatively good mood, given the severity of their survey and interview feedback. The manager wanted to give a presentation but agreed to see what staff could come up with first. Through a structured exercise, people came to realize that the drivers of change were external; clients, partners, and current events put new demands on their organization. Change was being driven by environmental factors, not by an uncaring leader. Throughout the day the manager encouraged others to air their concerns. At the close of the day, he acknowledged that he had been worried the off-site would be a gripe session. Now he had a sense of great optimism about their future. He wanted everyone to know there were no taboos in raising a topic or asking a question. His apparent willingness to hear dissent and concerns set a new tone of openness in the organization.

**Reflections:** While no one should claim Ron's shift in attitude led to the shift in his client's leadership style, it does suggest that synchronicity underlies the consultant/client or leader/group relationship. What we resist in others or our group, however justified, says more about us than we realize. The door to self-awareness and the use of self is humility. Humility enables us to see the connection between our judgments and our own limitations. It takes a strong and confident leader to ensure that speaking truth to power is part of the corporate culture. Just one sharp rebuke over someone's "inconvenient truth" could reinstate the attitude of cynicism and the norm of caution. In their interactions before the retreat, the facilitator, in his use of self, modeled for the manager a more productive way to engage with his staff around controversial topics. The off-site demonstrated in real time that disagreement can be done in a manner that safeguards the dignity of all concerned.

## Chapter 3
# Second Pillar:
# Systems Thinking

J ohn Muir never heard of systems thinking but he summed up the essence of it when he mused, "*When we try to pick out anything by itself, we find it hitched to everything else in the universe.*" Anything made up of component parts is a system. An organization is a system because it is a combination of interrelated people, groups, ideas, materials, and processes that exist in time and space. Systems thinking has its roots in the general system theory conceptualized by Austrian biologist Ludwig von Bertalanffy and others in the 1940s.[1] When a system works, the parts together create synergy; the "greater than" is generated by the relationships between those different parts.[2] The health of those relationships determines the size of the greater than.

One of my first steps whenever I work with an organization is to assess how its system and the component parts relate. I learn about the various departments or teams, the front office, and how work is brought in and flows through the organization. Key questions include what is the purpose of the organization and how is success defined and measured? From the system's perspective, I want to know what disrupts the relationships between those different parts and the collective goals they are trying to achieve. And, how can those relationships be improved or restored so that knowledge and other resources flow in an optimal manner? These questions uncover the baseline for the quality of interaction within the system.

Although this baseline is helpful in restoring productivity and harmony, it is insufficient. Creating a visual representation opens a deeper understanding. When an idea moves from the conceptual to the tangible, it uncovers more levels of meaning. Imagine, for example, a list of rising average temperatures for a mountainous region and compare that with satellite images showing the shrinking snow cover over time. Which one has a more visceral and personal impact? The term for this is "systems visualization." Instead of thinking about the system, a visual image of it is constructed using people or props.

John Curtis Gowan, an educational psychologist and the author of *Trance, Art and Creativity*, believed our ability to work with images underlies human progress. He wrote that *"In the case of every historic scientific discovery and invention that is researched carefully enough, we find that it was imagery, either in dreams or in a waking state, which produced the breakthrough."*[3] Images, and the feelings they evoke, are one way the vast intelligence of the collective unconscious communicates with the conscious mind. The power of an image is reflected in Aristotle's comment, "The soul never thinks without a picture." Using representatives in a constellation forms an image of the system being explored. That image changes as representatives move about and verbal phrases are introduced. Making things, ideas, or relationships more tangible and visible is a catalyst for learning. The dynamics of even a complex system can be quickly mapped using people or symbols. Those dynamics often reveal that the underlying systemic issue is not isolated in one person or department. The component parts of a business system commonly mapped with representatives include:

- ❒ Client as an individual or group
- ❒ Goal, desired outcome, or question
- ❒ Issue, challenge, or problem
- ❒ Purpose or vision of the organization
- ❒ Various departments, groups, or teams
- ❒ Obstacles or hidden agenda

Other parts that may be identified when mapping the system include:

- ❒ Founder(s)
- ❒ Management
- ❒ Staff or workers
- ❒ Mentors and supporters
- ❒ Processes and workflow
- ❒ Products, services, and success indicators
- ❒ Clients, stakeholders, partners, and regulators
- ❒ Different options or solutions

Not all these components need to be named and placed in a constellation. Usually, five or fewer are enough to clarify the issues and provide insights that lead to a solution. Creating a tangible representation of an intangible idea generates insights because the emotions and intuition become involved. The representation makes visible what was subconscious and hidden from view. What is too often characterized as a person problem—some lack of character or competence—is often structural and/or systemic. The resolution of a structural issue tends to be located in the present. For a systemic issue the resolution may have something to do with how we see the world based on past events.

W. Edwards Deming, of Total Quality Management (TQM) fame, tells a story of the CEO of a company with a pressing fire safety issue. He sent his 10,500 employees a letter pleading for them to be more careful with the highly flammable chemicals they handled.[4] The problem, from his perspective, was that employees were being negligent. The number of fires were eventually reduced, but only when structural changes in how those materials were handled were introduced. From a systemic perspective, what seemed to be a culture of carelessness was really a symptom of the CEO's careless reasoning. Mistaking a situational issue for a people problem is what Stanford psychologist Lee Ross calls a "fundamental attribution error."[5]

Defining a problem as a people problem makes it more difficult to talk about. A problem that cannot be talked about in a public setting is one that can't be solved. When the elephant is fleshed out in living color in front of everyone, that spell is broken. Physically mapping a system without preconceptions can reveal how the unseen, unacknowledged, or excluded parts of a system impact everyone in it. A common example of this is the failure to remember and honor the founders of an organization after they have retired. This lapse weakens the culture that made their company successful. Making an idea tangible enables the issue holder to see the problem from a number of different and more objective perspectives. She can walk around the representatives and notice as an outsider what is going on with each part and how that impacts the system as a whole. If *"you can see a lot by looking,"* as Yogi Berra famously said, you can see even more by looking from different perspectives. This shift in perspective for the seer often means the object being perceived shifts as well. "Seeing" phenomenologically has its roots in the word "shaman." The anthropologist Audrey Butt, during her fieldwork in the Amazon, reported that one of the Akawaio titles for a shaman was *eneogie, "the one who perceives."*[6]

## The System Remembers

Many organizations have a long history. Details and specifics that may have affected or caused the current issue are often forgotten as people retire or leave. What happened could be far enough back in the past that no one from that era is still employed or even living. Yet, the passage of time is not always a solution. Part of the system still remembers and can show up as:

❐ Systemic and persistent symptoms of the problem
❐ Source of the problem or trauma
❐ Excluded people—victims and perpetrators
❐ Secret or hidden agenda and benefit
❐ Coping or compensatory behaviors

Even though the details of an old trauma are lost, its impact can linger. Identifying that troubled past is a step toward the solution. Because what the client knows first-hand is often sketchy, the facilitator develops a hypothesis and then sets up representatives to test it. How the representatives respond to the setup and the emotional weight of what is revealed gives feedback as to its validity. Every frame of the setup is viewed phenomenologically. A representative takes action and then its impact is assessed. Acknowledging someone who was forgotten or overlooked can have a restorative effect on others. A common work-place drama is the lingering impact of a layoff. The part of the workforce that stays can be affected by survivor's guilt. Their morale and productivity suffer until the sacrifice of those laid off is seen and acknowledged. In difficult cases like this the solution may not be in the physical realm. It may come from the expanded intelligence of the knowing field, which has the capacity, when accessed, to reveal words and actions that mitigate the effects of the traumatic event. The saying "The answer is in the room" is true on many levels.

## Organizational Breakdowns

Most people need to spend but a few years in the work-force to witness firsthand an organization's numerous break-downs and shortcomings. Even a high-performing organization will have gone through or be going through some of the typical breakdowns listed below. The difference between a healthy organization and one that is not is the willingness to confront the breakdown when it arises. Open and frank discussion over time sustains the progress toward resolving the issue.

&#10065; ***Ethics and Integrity:*** The calamities that struck down companies like Enron or Worldcom were self-inflicted. There are systemic reasons why people who should know better do things that eventually catch up with them. The systemic factors that can either mitigate or enable a dysfunctional corporate culture are discussed in chapter 6 ("The Orders of Organizations").

&#10065; ***Commitment and Clarity:*** It does not matter if the purpose, mission, goals, roles, and processes are clear and viable when commitment is lacking.

If commitment is present but clarity is absent then progress could be in the wrong direction. The unifying impact of a clear and compelling purpose is evident in a number of the constellations presented in chapter 10 ("Organizational Constellations").

❏ *Resistance to Change:* There is a tendency to give lip service to the need for change while expecting the latest change initiative to fade just like the other management fads that were half-heartedly implemented and then forgotten. The insights of a change consultant who faced this situation are outlined in the case study "Cultural Innovation" in chapter 10.

❏ *Letting Go of What Was:* Resistance to change can arise in management as well as staff for reasons that might not be anticipated. The case study "Survivor's Guilt" (see chapter 10) indicates that the stages of grief defined by Elisabeth Kübler-Ross can also apply to a corporation going through drastic change.

❏ *Failure to Thrive:* The group's performance never reaches or exceeds the industry standard. The group might reorganize or change leaders, but the same questions about their ability, viability, and ROI still dog them. How one senior manager sought to inspire a sense of urgency without fostering panic is detailed in chapter 10 in the case study "International Ping Pong."

❏ *Silos:* The structural disconnection between groups or individuals in an organization is exasperated by the global nature of the business world. Blocks to the flow of information lead to duplications of effort and reinventing the wheel. The case study "Cross-Sector Change Management" in chapter 10 looks at ways to reduce those barriers in a geographically diverse workplace.

❑ ***Them versus Us:*** The most fundamental of all projections is the perception of one group versus another. This is so hardwired in Western culture that if you take a group and divide it temporarily into two groups for an exercise, they will almost always compete, ignore, or discount each other. Management versus staff, the field versus headquarters, one department against another—all are prone to the "blame game" as shown in the case study "New Messages for a New Plan" in chapter 12 ("Management Constellations").

❑ ***Hostile Workplace:*** This is usually thought to be caused by a leader who abuses his or her power and bullies subordinates. However, a tone of gossip and general fault finding by staff members can also foster a fractured workplace and low morale. Systemic sources such as the victim/perpetrator dynamic may be the hidden source of the dysfunction, as is revealed in the case study "The Hidden Sources of Conflict" in chapter 15 ("Professional Constellations").

Other case studies are related to the following archetypes, which also contribute to organizational breakdowns and shortcomings:

❑ ***Personality Conflicts:*** Personality conflicts lack a logical explanation so people pin the conflict on different styles even though those differences are trivial. The conflict actually represents a symptom, not a cause. When the systemic source of a conflict is surfaced and acknowledged, the possibility of reconciliation is enhanced.

❑ **Analysis Paralysis:** The more educated and articulate the group, the more likely they are to trip themselves up by making things too complex. One way to avoid an endless mix of pros, cons, what-ifs, and tangential asides is described in the case study "Type-A Paralysis" in chapter 17 ("Just in Time Constellating").

❑ **Disruptive Employees:** They may get their work done, but they can be difficult to work with and even more difficult to manage. For various bureaucratic reasons, no HR actions can be or will be taken. How this type of breakdown was dealt with systemically is detailed in the case study "Things Are Not Always as They Seem" in chapter 17.

Research by the Gallup Group shows that a simple and specific thank-you for a job well done, along with a greeting like good morning, fosters greater employee engagement.[7] Something so simple and effective, quick and free should be in every manager's repertoire. When those textbook actions don't help and the problem becomes urgent, then it's wise to look for a systemic solution. The systemic approach outlined in the case studies I cross-referenced in the preceding lists is the leadership tool of last resort that people turn to when everything else has failed.

Using the computer metaphor once more, if you can find and correct the errors in the source code, the dysfunctions on the screen will be resolved. The hidden component of change resides in the unconscious beliefs that have a systemic impact. Behind the organizational breakdown is a broken order of the organization that can be traced back to a fault-inducing trauma or belief. A skillfully facilitated constellation will provide a visible image of the dysfunctional beliefs or traumatic impressions hidden in the individual's or group's subconscious. Once the issue holder finds and names those impressions, he or she can test various solutions to see if they restore the connection between the parts of the system, enabling vital information to flow freely.

## Business as Usual

A common concern about a change initiative is that after the retreat is over, people fall back into the same unconscious and unproductive routines. A month or two later they complain that nothing has changed. Even if there have been positive changes, distraction and disengagement keep many from noticing. Action plans and agreements are necessary but not enough. A deeper level of intervention is needed to affect change at the source, which is the collective unconscious of the group. Working with the knowing field illuminates the underlying causes that drive the systemic challenges and conflicts in the workplace. It also identifies the resources and solutions that will address those challenges in a sustainable manner.

## No Going Back

Oliver Wendell Holmes famously said, "A mind, once expanded by a new idea, never returns to its original dimensions."[8] When a person or a group accesses some part of their individual or collective subconscious, the stretching that occurs can't be rescinded. Consciousness is like a container: as we expand the container and clarify the contents, more knowledge can be held and understood. The Vedic mystic Sri Nisargadatta Maharaj explains what happens when we bring the unconscious parts of us to awareness:

*We are slaves to what we do not know; of what we know we are masters. Whatever vice or weakness in ourselves (if) we discover and understand its causes and workings, we overcome it by the very knowing; the unconscious dissolves when brought to the conscious.*[9]

The process of expanding self-awareness requires self-observation and reflection. This is not a comfortable undertaking, yet no one else can do it for you. But, according to Carl Jung, *"Until you make the unconscious conscious it will direct your life and you will call it fate."*

## Chapter 4
# Third Pillar:
# The Knowing Field

Reality has two aspects. The first is objective. We interact with our world and something happens in space and time. The second is subjective. Our mind interprets what happened and assigns meaning and emotions to the event. The conscious and subconscious parts of our mind cocreate with others the objective and subjective aspects of the world we experience.

## Awareness and Cocreated Reality

Most people are familiar with the metaphor of an iceberg and its application to how we interact with the world. What is below the waterline, our threshold of awareness, is much greater than what is above. The model in Figure 4-1 divides our consciousness into three levels.

The first level, cocreated reality, is something we are naturally conscious of. In the second level we are aware of some, but not fully all, of the actions, thoughts, feelings,

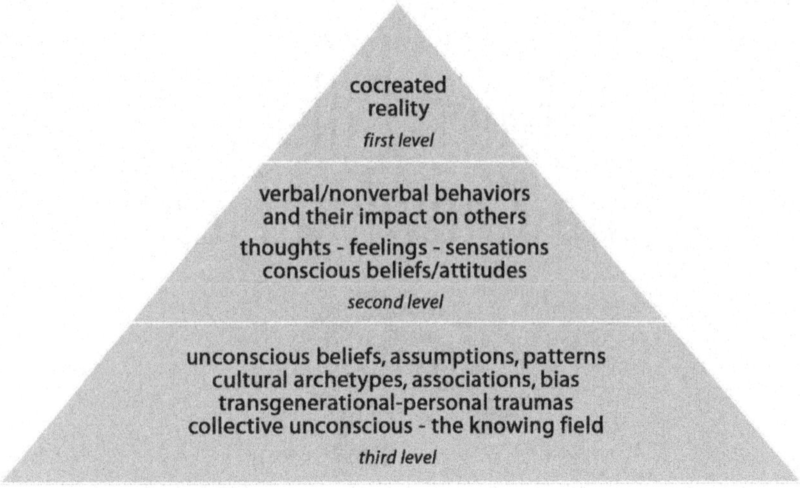

**Figure 4-1: The Iceberg Model of Awareness**

and sensations that give rise to that reality. Within our sub-conscious, at the third level, there is a vast realm of impressions and beliefs we are only vaguely aware of, if at all. As a multilevel, non-lateral problem-solving tool, the constellation process accesses these three levels. This process is based on the following assumptions:

- ❐ Our reality is cocreated.
- ❐ Our inner experience determines to a great extent our outer experience.
- ❐ The second and third levels of consciousness determine how we shape and respond to an experience cocreated on the first level.
- ❐ A significant part of our inner experience—some of the second level and most of the third—are below the threshold of awareness.
- ❐ Bringing those hidden, excluded, denied, or forgotten parts to awareness fosters more self-awareness and consequently more opportunity to shape our outer experience through conscious choices.

❐ Seeking feedback, counseling, or coaching and practicing personal reflection and self-observation foster more awareness of the second level of behaviors, thoughts, and feelings.

❐ The impact of past traumas can be transferred between generations through epigenetics and affect the other two levels.

❐ Conducting a family or professional constellation will bring more awareness of material hidden in the third level, mitigating the impact it has on the other levels.

## Kissing Your Frog

The first movement in transforming our personal reality is taking responsibility for the impact our other levels of consciousness have in shaping it. The flow of this process is diagrammed in the structure of a typical constellation as shown in Figure 4-2. If we agree that our personal reality is impacted, if not determined, by our second and third levels of consciousness then we are ready to do something about that reality. Letting go of assigning blame and stepping out of the victim-perpetrator dynamic enables us to work with the part of the system we have influence or control over: ourselves. Kissing your frog, defined here as the "Transformation Through Systemic Mapping Model," starts at the top left side at Level 1 of Consciousness. It moves down to Level 3 then across to Visible Resources on the right and then up to the Desired Reality. The Current Reality, or "what is" corresponds to the first and second levels of consciousness of the issue holder. The constellation can reveal material in the third level of consciousness that the issue holder was not unaware of.

Keeping in mind the desired outcome articulated by the issue holder, the facilitator looks for and tests the

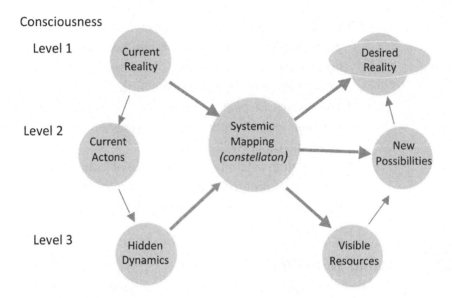

Consciousness

**Figure 4-2: Transformation Through Systemic Mapping**

Hidden Dynamics at Level 3, within the subconscious, that
are influencing the other two levels. Identifying and bringing those dynamics or traumas to conscious awareness
help transform a hidden obstacle into a visible resource.
The light of awareness generates insights that free up
misdirected energy. As the flow moves upward from
resources, participants may notice an energetic shift that
indicates something changed at the subconscious level.
This change supports the desired outcome, which feels
more realistic and attainable. No one should claim that a
constellation automatically provides a person with his or
her desired reality. Skillfully facilitated, however, the constellation should offer a map of the desired outcome linked
to actions, resources, and insights that correspond to the
second and third levels of consciousness.

## Accessing the Knowing Field

During a constellation, information is surfaced that leads to new insights and possibilities. The process works by taking intangible mental concepts and giving them a physical and an emotional representation. Information does often emerge, however, that only the issue holder is privy to. Surprised by what has been revealed people want to understand how this happened. The short answer is we really don't know. One possible explanation is that we are all connected to an "energetic internet" we will call the knowing field. When the representatives in a constellation quiet their verbal mind, they nurture the connection between their nonverbal subconscious mind and the infinite knowing field of all subconscious minds. The endless possibilities of this collective field can provide us with unexpected revelations. Since the information is coming through the subconscious it tends to be a felt-sense of physical and emotional sensations. This felt-sense phenomenologically describes the issue and the solutions that would lead to its resolution.

A simple exercise offers a visceral insight into how we naturally access this field of knowing. Ask people to sit next to someone they have not yet met. Ask them to write down five characteristics of the new person and five characteristics about themselves on separate notecards. They should do this before they start talking to each other. When they both have finished, ask them to share what they wrote about each other and themselves. Generally, people find the shared cards to be surprisingly accurate even though the writers had very little overt information to go on. Somehow, accurate information was available even though they were not aware of any physical source.

What if the members of your group already know each other? Another approach for this personal research project is to ask the participants to form triads. One person will be the experimenter and the other two will be the subjects. The experimenters think of someone with whom they have an intense relationship. The relationship could be positive or negative—but not so negative they feared for their safety. The experimenters select one of the subjects to represent themselves and the other subject to represent the person who is in the intense relationship. Without telling the subjects whom they represent, the experimenters position the pairs a few feet apart. The experimenters then touch each subject on the shoulder with the quiet intention in mind of who that subject represents. The subjects are given a few minutes to notice what they notice without any agenda. Then they report how they feel about each other. Again, experimenters find the representatives' comments are surprisingly accurate. One explanation is that through mirror neurons in the brain we sense what others are feeling. The reaction time, according to some brain researchers, in sensing whether someone is a friend or foe is a mere .07 seconds.[1] As neuroscience uncovers more about the capacity of the human brain, we will continue to be amazed by what our neurology can do.

## Being Your Own Scientist

The knowing field is not located in the individual mind. Yet, the individual mind can be used to explore the field. One way to start this exploration is to use systems thinking to map out the component parts of the problem or question posed by the issue holder. This is where you make good use of your mental powers; a systems analysis starts with forming a picture of the issue. The details are teased out by asking: What are the parts of the system? How do they relate to each other? What needs to happen to restore harmony or order?

The next step is to send your verbal mind on a break and let your body, emotions, and spirit or intuition take the stage. According to the *Wall Street Journal*, brain researchers peg the number of calculations that the conscious brain can work on at the same time at one. In comparison, the simultaneous activities in unconscious parts of the brain number in the billions.[2] The conscious mind tries to make sense of things through comparisons, judgments, and categories: this is good, that is bad, and so forth. Staying in the brain's mental mode, one calculation at a time, can limit access to a much larger field of intelligence and knowing that is contacted through the subconscious. I often tell groups, especially those new to the systemic approach, that what we are doing is not conceptual. The analytical process has its place and time, just not everywhere 24/7.

The rational mind is eager to know and will quickly make up stories and explanations to fill a void. It tends to not slow down enough to decipher the memo from the unconscious that has the answers it seeks. Accessing the tacit knowledge that resides in our subconscious is possible if we tolerate the discomfort of emptiness and uncertainty our conscious mind runs from.

## Taking a "Field" Trip

According to Lynne McTaggart, author of *The Field: The Quest for the Secret Force of the Universe*, a field is *"a region of influence...a medium that connects two or more points in space."*[3] Objects in a field are influenced by it and by each other through a connection or force that is not visible to the eye. McTaggart quotes a number of scientists who believe that the zero point field, the field of all fields, is a vast storehouse of memory. The biologist Rupert Sheldrake postulated that fields have a morphic resonance that influences how those living within them look and act.

He asserts that all living beings are shaped by *"a living, developing universe with its own inherent memory."*[4] The nature of the world and the beings in it is determined by this field of fields. According to Einstein, *"The field is the ultimate reality."*

So how do we connect with this ultimate reality of infinite potential? McTaggart reports the findings of researchers that *"the unconscious mind somehow had the capacity of communicating with the sub-tangible physical world."*[5] The unconscious and the zero point field exist together *"in a probabilistic state of all possibilities."*[6] The details of how this works are a mystery. We only know that it is possible to access this field through the nonverbal subconscious and that we temporarily experience the reality of other individuals or groups.

Every living system has its own collective consciousness. The connection between each individual consciousness in a living system constitutes a field. Most of what is in the field exists below the threshold of human awareness. You might not be aware of all the forces that shape your behaviors and attitudes, but they affect you in more ways than it's possible to comprehend. The social psychologist Karl Weick made an intriguing point that the word "organization" is *"a myth. If you look for an organization you won't find one. What you will find is...connected incidents that seep through concrete walls..."*[7] Connected incidents, especially ones that can seep through a wall unconstrained by time or space, is the classic definition of a field.

Einstein referred to this unified field when he said, *"All religions, arts and sciences are branches of the same tree."* Our mind, body, and spirit, along with everything else in the manifest world, are all expressions of one infinitely pulsating consciousness. When we tap into the zero point field, according to McTaggart, we tap into all possibilities.[8]

Everything comes out and goes back to the nothing-
ness of the zero point. This is not news. Ancient texts like
the Upanishads have long professed the interconnected-
ness of all life. Recent research published by NASA phys-
icists postulates that the universe is about 27 percent dark
matter and 68 percent dark energy. The remaining 5 percent
is the world of physical matter that we can actually see (1.5
percent) or measure in some way (3.5 percent).[9] NASA is
basically telling us that comprehending the universe goes
beyond the capacities of the human mind. In other words,
life is a lot weirder than we can even imagine. If the 170
billion observable galaxies are just a small fraction of our
universe, where is the rest of it?

These figures are in line with the mystical perspective
of the kabbalah. It states that we only experience 1 percent of reality on the Earth dimension. The rest of reality,
the 99 percent we don't perceive, is in what is called the
"Upper World." Native Americans from the Sioux Nation
use the expression "Wakan Tanka," the Great Mystery, to
refer to the vastness of creation that is more than mankind
can hope to understand. Despite the immensity of all the
unknown, according to the astrophysicist Neil DeGrasse
Tyson, mankind does have a place. One possibility is that
*"We are a way for the Cosmos to know itself."* [10] Our awareness and the awareness binding together the mysteries of
the universe are of the same fabric.

## Everyday Mind

Though the vastness of the zero point field is heady
stuff, from day to day your conscious mind fills your head
with a stream of mundane thoughts. Those thoughts are
often observations, judgments, fears, and desires related
to the future or the past. According to David Rock, a neuroscience expert, our everyday mind is so noisy it is difficult

to hear ourselves think. When the ego is identified with the everyday mind, that constant stream of verbal thought gives it a sense of security. Quieting the mind is difficult because the ego wants to hold on to what it knows. I've noticed in my consulting work that the smarter and more educated a group is, the more susceptible they are to the trap of analysis paralysis. In that trap are verbal knots of convoluted logic and assertions that sound erudite but actually mean that nothing will be decided or acted on. One way out is to have the group engage for a few minutes in some physical or nonverbal activity. A quiet mind increases the capacity for holistic self-observation; noticing what is happening physically, emotionally, and spiritually. And self-observation by an individual or a group, according to Ray Bradbury, leads to change-inducing insights. Paradoxically, this kind of self-observation is possible when people are not overwhelmed by their own self-conscious and self-absorbed mental activity.

## Can an Organization Have a Soul?

No one has proven objectively that you have a soul, so why ask such a question about a man-made construct like an organization? There is reason to ask. When a personal consciousness identifies with others, it helps form a collective consciousness. This collective does not have the traits of free will. It is more like an energetic field. This energetic field is nonphysical, yet somehow it contains information about the group, its culture and level of well-being, that can be accessed nonverbally. Think of the times you have walked into an office and sensed the mood of the people who worked there. That exchange of information can be two ways. For instance, after visiting an office where morale was either intensely low or festive your mood was affected accordingly. The emotions and mood of the group, even those unexpressed, were contagious.

Sidestepping the issues of an afterlife, there are many secular ways to interpret the word "soul." Bert Hellinger, who developed the constellation methodology for use with family systems, makes a distinction between a personal soul and the "greater soul." We will discuss Hellinger's contribution to this methodology in greater detail in chapter 5 ("Accessing Tacit Knowledge"). Till then, the soul, according to Hellinger, is not something we possess; *"rather, it is something that connects us in a community with others, in ever greater circles... [linking] us with a shared wisdom and...the pursuit of a common goal."* [11] John Ortberg has a similar belief that *"the soul is what integrates separate functions into a single, organic whole..."* [12] While Ortberg is referring to individuals, change facilitators know that groups have an inner drive toward integration. The role of the facilitator is clear: resolve the misperceptions that block the integration of the discordant parts into a harmonious whole. At the end of a successful meeting or off-site event, the positive energy that embraces the group is a reflection of this innate drive toward integration.

# Chapter 5
# Accessing Tacit Knowledge

The foundation of the corporate shaman approach is based on a methodology called "family constellations." Bert Hellinger developed this methodology by combining the two complementary approaches to problem-solving, analysis and synthesis, in a way that was embodied and multidimensional. The parts of a problem identified through analysis were made tangible by assigning them physical representation. The synthesis of the parts was facilitated through the interactions of the representatives. Making their relationships tangible brought more perspectives to the issue. This, in turn, uncovered solutions that had been excluded by the limitations of a single point of view. Hellinger drew upon his experiences living with the Zulus in South Africa as a missionary for sixteen years. The parallels between his methodology and the ceremonies of indigenous people has been remarked upon by many. For instance, when Francesca Mason Boring, a Native American facilitator, was introduced to the process, she remarked, *"It was very familiar to me because it reminded me of Cree ceremonial traditions."* [1]

In addition to indigenous sources, Hellinger reportedly drew inspiration from the therapeutic community, including Eric Berne's Transactional Analysis and "the discovery that some scripts function across generations." It is interesting that the Austrian-born philosopher and educator Rudolf Steiner, who founded the Waldorf Schools, had a similar perspective about how people are influenced by their lineage. "Separate individuals are merely the executive organs of these family soul groups." [2]

## Defining Our Terms

Hellinger called his process of mapping a family system a constellation, evoking the patterns formed by stars. Family constellations address personal issues that affect a person's life and well-being. The presenting issue is often related to some difficulty or trauma in a person's family of origin. The process of mapping reveals the expanded circle of influence within the family system. In this expanded circle the deceased members, as well as the living, have an impact on the issue holder.

The term "family constellations" refers to a method for identifying patterns of human behavior. This method has evolved substantially over the past few years. What started out as a way to uncover the dynamics within a family system was adapted by business professionals to explore the dynamics within an organizational system.

This adaption occurred when Hellinger was asked to help several business leaders understand and address the challenges their companies faced. While the work proved successful, Hellinger felt his primary focus was on family and individual development. He invited Gunther Weber, a German medical doctor who had studied constellations with him, to take the lead in responding to the growing interest from the business community. Because of Dr. Weber's early and extensive involvement facilitating constellations for businesses groups in the 1990s and later, he became known as the father of organizational constellations. In countries like Germany, Austria, Holland, and parts of Scandinavia, the methodology gained acceptance and recognition as one of the tools a business consultant, coach, or therapist might use when working with a client.

The terminology used to label these adaptions over time became more precise. Business-related constellations were described as: systemic, structural, organizational, management, and professional. The definitions below are offered to clarify these terms and show where they overlap. Because this is a new and an evolving field with no official keeper of terminology, it's possible the diligent student will come across definitions that differ from the ones that follow.

***Systemic Constellations:*** All constellations are systemic in that they seek to identify and acknowledge the underlying causes of a particular issue. The issue and its cause are not always readily apparent in the framework of the family or organizational system. Each element in the system has its place. The impact of an element that is missing or excluded cannot be avoided. The systemic approach is used to reveal the hidden dynamics and dysfunctions in any system, be it family or a work group, and develop solutions that bring the system back to a state of balance. The key elements of the system can be people, concepts, or things. They are considered key if they play a major role in the issue or challenge being explored. They are represented either by a person, an object, or a label. The parts that are identified during the initial conversation between the facilitator and the issue holder are used to create a map of the system that uniquely reflects the dynamics of that particular collection of parts.

***Structural Constellations:*** Matthias Varga von Kibéd, a professor at the University of Munich, and his wife, Insa Sparrer, a psychotherapist, founded the SySt Institute. They were influential in the development of specialized formats for the constellation process.[3] Structural constellations, unlike their systemic cousins, have a predetermined format that organizes in advance how the representatives will be selected and arranged. Examples of a structural format are the resource constellation or the work/life balance constellations described in chapter 15 ("Professional Constellations").

***Organizational Constellations:*** An organizational constellation explores and addresses business issues related to an organization. The process can be conducted for individuals in an open enrollment workshop or with a group that belongs to the same organization. The issue holder is someone who wants insight into a business challenge or question. Anonymity is easier to maintain at an open enrollment workshop because the people attending usually do not know each other and can keep their organization and roles confidential. Chapter 10 ("Organizational Constellations") explains how these constellations are facilitated.

***Management Constellations:*** This is an organizational constellation conducted with an intact work group on a work-related topic. The constellation offers a graphic way of breaking a complex system or issue into its parts so the dynamics within that system are better understood. Because of the lack of anonymity in an intact working group, management constellations tend to focus on strategic or external issues that are more open to public analysis. Care is taken to deal appropriately with individual attitudes and feelings that could compromise or embarrass one or more group members. It's always wise to get to know the group and the sensitivities of the members before launching into a constellation. Chapter 12 ("Management Constellations") presents case studies of some of the management constellations I have done with work groups.

***Professional Constellations:*** In an open enrollment workshop the participants bring specific concerns related to their work and career. Their questions revolve around such issues as working with a difficult boss or coworker, uncertainty about taking a job, or challenges around launching or managing a business. Not infrequently, the challenges explored in a professional constellation are found to be linked to an unresolved or a neglected issue in the issue holder's family of origin. The issue holder is given the option of going deeper to resolve the family issue or postponing this exploration for a more private setting. Just being aware of this linkage can be enough to lead to a resolution over time. Chapter 15 ("Professional Constellations") contains a number of case studies that focus on professional issues.

## Phenomenological Work

Systemic facilitation is phenomenological as opposed to theoretical. This means the facilitator works with what is showing up in the issue holder's constellation and the impact of the issue holder's choices and actions. The dynamics described by the issue holder guide the initial setup of the representatives. When a representative moves or makes a statement or the issue holder speaks about the situation, notice the effect that has in the room. Is the energy raised or lowered? Does the representative feel better or worse? Notice the affect embodied in the present moment and observe the body language and tone of voice of the representatives.

The seemingly rational mind is often influenced by assumptions and beliefs that lead to faulty conclusions. Bias tricks us into confusing opinions for facts. What is expressed subconsciously and nonverbally through the body does not mislead. Body language always tells the truth. Just take a moment to quiet the mind and notice.

Hellinger makes a useful distinction between observing and seeing. *"The word 'observing' means observing individual details at the cost of the perception of the whole. When I see persons...I grasp what is essential about them."*[4] Seeing holistically is a function of the "beginners mind": that is, the part of the seer that is free of ulterior motives and preconceptions. *"Seeing means that I open myself completely to complex connections and allow them to work in me, to affect me."*[5]

Facilitating phenomenologically is seeing and observing what is showing up in the present moment. Doing both enables the facilitator to feel within him- or herself what has been said or done and connect it to where it makes sense. That connection takes the form of a hypothesis, which is then tested through trial and error. These tests include re-positioning the representatives or providing phrases they repeat. The physical, emotional, or spiritual changes that occur may lead to insights that surprise the rational mind. The issue holder and the representatives will sense immediately if an insight or resolution has been gained. The facilitator holds the overview of the system, namely, what needs to happen and the options for achieving this resolution. The representatives are too engaged in the process to maintain this objective overview. As needed, some facilitators will step into a place of subjectivity by entering and exiting the system as a temporary representative. Briefly standing in the flow of energy between the representatives provides another level of information. Something new emerges as an insight or energetic shift. It is felt by everyone in the room, and it gives a sense of completion that what needed to happen, happened.

### The Fourth Quadrant

Since the 1960s the Johari Window, developed by psychologists Joseph Luft and Harry Ingham in 1955, has been part of many leadership development programs.[6] It is used as a model to explain self-awareness, a key leadership competency. There are four quadrants to the model (see Figure 5-1). The first three—Open, Blind, and Hidden Self—are expanded by the conscious mind through reflection, sharing information, or asking for feedback. The fourth quadrant, the Unknown Self, is where both you and others are in the dark. You don't know what is there and neither do they.

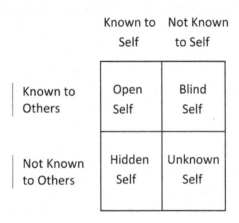

**Figure 5-1: Johari Window**

No doubt you've heard someone say, "Why did I do that? I knew it was not a good idea." The missing piece of self-knowledge in this unfortunate scenario hides out in the Unknown Self. This is your subconscious, the untapped part of yourself which holds tremendous growth potential. The trick is in gaining access. As the saying goes, the problem with the unconscious is that it is unconscious. The bigger the shadow cast by the Unknown Self, the more likely it is you will get in your own way or be overwhelmed by complexity. One method to reduce the size of that shadow is through a constellation. Other methods include dream analysis, hypnotherapy, Gestalt, and therapeutic art, to name a few. Many gifted therapists or coaches can tap directly into a person's subconscious or the collective consciousness of a group.[7] In a constellation the intuitive powers of the facilitator are helpful, but they are not the most active ingredient. The structure of the constellation is the force driving the process. This ability to access an energetic field of knowing is innate. People have it by virtue of being human. They just need the organizing skill and guidance the facilitator provides.

# Chapter 6

# The Orders of Organizations

I f organizations are living systems with dynamic relationships between their parts then it stands to reason those parts would interact based on systemic principles. These principles, or "orders," subconsciously shape behaviors in an instinctive manner that transcends cultures and industries. Understanding the orders gives you, the leader or consultant, a tool for assessing the soul of the organization. They help reveal the unconscious factors that lie behind the dynamics playing out between individuals and groups. When the orders are in place, the flow of information within the system is less hindered. When the orders are out of place, specific phrases and physical movements can be used to optimize the flow of information and restore harmony.

## The Systemic Detective

Our approach to problem-solving often treats the symptom instead of the underlying cause. Resistant and reoccurring symptoms are often part of a long-standing pattern. The tip-off is when a client uses the words "always" or "never." Statements like, "I always end up with an abusive boss" or "Clients never appreciate my work" may indicate that a systemic issue is shaping the issue holder's reality. The workplace may change and the people in it but the same pattern will keep showing up until the underlying cause is surfaced and addressed.

## Organizational Orders

In the family constellation system, according to Hellinger, there is a natural hierarchy and flow of energy he called *orders of love*.[1] These "orders" are hardwired patterns of human behavior that support the flow of love. Trauma and exclusion can disrupt the connections within the pattern and hinder the flow of love between generations. Unless the connections are restored or addressed in some way, problems arise that are systemic, far-reaching, and tragic. William Faulkner expressed that truth when he wrote, *"The past is never dead. It's not even past."* In fiction or real life, what happened in the past, even if it is forgotten or denied, can profoundly affect those who follow.

Organizations also follow the orders of love, with some meaningful differences. To differentiate these differences we will call this set of orders the *orders of organizations*. These are the subconscious templates that shape how people in an organization relate to their environment and each other. Harmony exists when the dynamics of the orders are maintained and supported. Harmony is disrupted when those dynamics are disturbed. Restoring the connections within the pattern restores the system as a whole.

Like the above "orders," the skill sets for facilitating family or organizational constellations are similar. Obviously, family constellations focus on the family system while organizational constellations explore aspects of an organization. The starting point for both is identifying and setting up the key elements of the system. The space between those elements, their relationships and interdependencies, is observed and then worked with so as to restore balance and order. What differs is the tone of the session.

Delving into an organizational issue can be objective and impersonal if that is the nature of the problem. While there might be strong emotions present, they are less often felt in a deeply personal way. Becoming a world-class team is a worthy goal, but not one people usually shed tears of joy or pain over. Functions or things do not tend to feel emotions like people do. For example, during a constellation assessing the viability in the market of two different products, one of the products was shown to be much more viable than the other one was.

As the facilitator, I asked the representative for the less viable product how she felt about this assessment. She responded that she was a product and did not really have feelings about it one way or another. In a family constellation, if one sibling was preferred over another, it's likely that deep feelings will surface, especially if they had been long denied. This can come up in a constellation about a business issue, but usually it is not what the client put on the table. A skilled systemic facilitator should be adept in working with both family and organizational issues because in the organizational context one can lead to the other.

The orders of organizations include, but are not limited to, the following list of eleven workplace dynamics:

***Honoring the Founder:*** You may have noticed that in some companies there is a place in a public area with pictures and commentary about the company's founder. Although the company may have changed dramatically over time, its culture and defining values can still be traced back to its founder and the stories of his or her exploits. In systemic thinking the blessings of the founder are transferred to the successor in the same way the blessings of a parent are transferred to a child when the child honors the parent. Forgetting to acknowledge the founder weakens the vision and values that hold the employees together as a company. The case study "Gripping the Purse" in chapter 11 ("Family Business Challenges") illustrates the systemic dynamics behind the transition of power from one generation to the next.

Ignoring or forgetting the core values and vision of the founder can put a company at risk. Companies like Arthur Anderson, LLP, whose credibility and viability as one of the big five public accounting firms depended on adhering to its core principles, abruptly went out of business as a consequence of its forgetfulness. If those values had been remembered and followed it is less likely Anderson and its client, Enron, would have folded, resulting in 85,000 Anderson employees and 20,000 Enron employees losing their jobs and billions of dollars of shareholder value evaporating.[2]

***The Balance of Giving and Receiving:*** When someone gives something or does a favor for someone, the recipient often instinctively feels the need to give a gift or favor in return. The bonds of a relationship can be broken by this hidden sense of obligation: not by the person doing the giving, but by the person who has consistently received more than his share. The increasing sense of indebtedness becomes unsustainable and the relationship deteriorates or is broken off. In a similar fashion, employees have an unspoken agreement about what the balance of giving to the company and receiving in turn should be. Someone who gives either too little or too much relative to that unspoken norm disrupts the system. While people seldom complain that they are overpaid and underworked, they are acutely aware of those they perceive to be in that category. The greater the discrepancy, the more troubling it is to others since it runs counter to their sense of fairness and reciprocity. Employees who contribute less than the norm may not quit, but if the problem is not addressed they become angry and resentful and they withdraw as a way to justify their lack of contribution. This fosters a downward spiral toward more imbalance and disharmony. Organizations that make it difficult for management to hold staff accountable through layers of administrative regulation and oversight are prone to this phenomenon.

Frequently when I conduct leadership programs in a large organization, supervisors complain about this type of performance issue. It may look like the problem started with the employee's disengaged attitude, but in many cases the source was an imbalance in giving and receiving that the employee felt unable to correct. A related issue is the popular perception of North American CEOs as robber barons whose compensation by far exceeds their contribution. Regardless of the level in the hierarchy where it occurs, according to systemic thinking, inequities in the ratio of giving and receiving foster agitation and cynicism.

*The Hierarchy of Contribution:* Those who contribute more to the success of the company generally are afforded more status and greater rewards compared to others. Their contributions include highly valued technical skills, innovative ideas, good judgment, or new clients. As managers they take responsibility for the good of the whole. What makes life interesting in any organization, of course, are the crosscurrents of competing hierarchies. Many frictions between baby boomers and Gen Xers can be traced back to different levels of adherence to the principles of the "First Come First" and Belonging and Place," which are described below.

*The First Come First:* It used to be a given that those who had more seniority took precedence over those who had less. Boomers, who came of age between the mid-'60s and mid-'70s, and early Gen-Xers wonder why the later Gen-Xers and the Millennials seem so disinterested in "paying their dues." Younger staff feel that they are entitled to more decision-making authority than their older managers are willing to give them. They resent the expectation that they need to gain more experience and prove their competence before taking a seat in the boardroom. Tensions over working in a hierarchy that are actually generational can escalate into perceptions of ageism and gender or racial bias. When the younger staff habitually think and act as if they know better than their boss does, it disrupts the sense of order and role clarity. Their tacit acknowledgment that their boss is their boss and they are the employees can restore that clarity and order.

*The Right to Belong:* Everyone in a family has the right to belong. Hellinger believes this right cannot be taken away without consequences for the family.[3]

If someone is forgotten or rejected, then another member of the family system will unconsciously, in some manner, take on the fate of the excluded member. Organizations differ since people come and go. Belonging is not a right; it is given and can be taken away or given up. While the right to belong is not a given, people who have been long-standing members of an organization cannot be suddenly excluded without a serious impact on those who remain. That impact is exacerbated when someone is fired or laid off and no one acknowledges the employee's departure or provides sufficient cause. While the norm of confidentiality is a constraint, some context is needed when abrupt departures happen. If people are laid off in an effort to keep the company from folding, an acknowledgment of their sacrifice should be made. When nothing is said, those who stay feel the collective pain of an emotionally unsettled workplace. Those who keep their jobs when others are laid off may feel a sense of survivor's guilt. Making mistakes becomes a way to atone for their guilt. Their own sense of belonging is threatened because it appears it can be lost without due cause.

**Belonging and Place:** The need to belong is a primary human drive. Being an accepted member of a group gives us a sense of security and identity. Without the affirmation and structure of these groups most of us would not know who we are or where we should be. Even if we unequivocally identify with a group, confusion arises when we are uncertain of our place. In a family, conflict between siblings can arise when a younger sibling takes precedence over an older one. The natural order is that the older has more responsibility and authority than the younger does. When the older takes on the role of the rebellious child, the younger is likely to assume the role of the reliable child who takes precedence because he takes on more responsibility. Add in the family expectations around gender—a boy, even if the younger one, should have more freedom than should a girl, even if the older one—and resentments are likely to arise.

Conflicts in the workplace unfold in a similar way. When people accept their places and privileges in the hierarchy there is less anxiety or resentment. The matrix organization has advantages over layers or silos of hierarchy because of its flexibility in organizing resources around work priorities. Turf battles and professional rivalries, however, are likely to occur when it's not clear who makes what decision or even who is working for or with whom.

M. Scott Peck, psychiatrist and author of the best seller *The Road Less Traveled,* has a particularly telling story about when he was a commanding officer of a US Army medical unit. Influenced by the antiauthoritarian ideals of the '60s, then Major Scott was eager to mitigate the structural rigidity of military rank and file. Seeking to foster a more relaxed and collegial atmosphere he encouraged the officers and enlisted in his unit to use first names. Decisions were made by consensus. Briefly, morale soared, but then it began to slip and nothing Peck did seemed to help. One young soldier told him, *"I feel I don't know where I stand."* Frustrated with the bickering and poor performance, Scott finally took charge and began giving specific directions, starting with assigning each soldier his working space as part of an office move.[4] Restoring the sense of hierarchy and place might not have worked in Silicon Valley, but it was what Peck's unit needed to improve morale and performance given the experience level of his unit and the larger culture they were all part of. Scott's lack of success with participatory decision-making does not mean every group should avoid this style. Groups at different stages of development or engaged in different tasks need different styles of leadership. What might work for research scientists who have worked together for years may not work at all for a new team of firefighters.

*Physical Order:* Another aspect of place is where people stand or sit in relationship to each other. The reason the boss has the corner office is not just for the view. People position themselves according to their rank and status. The most senior sit at the head of the rectangular table and the less senior to their left.

Round tables, famously starting with the Knights of the Round Table in the days of King Arthur, mitigate the sense of hierarchy and encourage a more open exchange of views. Interestingly enough, in all my many years facilitating hundreds of meetings on-site in boardrooms in many parts of the world, I have yet to come across a round table. When the meeting is off-site at a conference center, round tables that accommodate six to ten participants tend to be the norm. My preference, as the facilitator, is to do away with the tables and simply put the chairs in a circle. In the military the senior person walks on the right, respecting an ancient tradition that allowed the senior person more access to his sword. Following this template that assigns each person his or her place can have a subtle, calming effect. Our subconscious notices when physical position and social status are in alignment or not. One way to experience the power of positioning is by doing the "Organogram Exercise" explained in chapter 19 ("Exploring the Field with Structured Exercises").

***Good Conscience and Tribal Loyalty:*** Western culture and education emphasize ethics and morality. Business school case studies stress the link between ethical lapses and business disasters. Yet, how do we explain why so many intelligent, highly educated leaders do unethical, even illegal, things with hardly a second thought? One rationale offered by the responsible parties when they are caught is that "everyone else was doing it." It's not grounds for an acquittal, but this excuse contains a certain truth. Our conscience monitors our degree of belonging to our group. Hellinger's insight was that we feel guilty when we do something that threatens that sense of belonging. Our conscience is clear when our actions conform to our group's norms.[5]

People can do terrible things to others with a clear conscience when their group condones or encourages those actions. The unconscious drive to belong can trump the internal constraints that might preclude illegal or unethical behavior. The group conscience outweighs individual conscience. It takes self-awareness and courage to leave or take on the tenuous role of whistleblower. The shenanigans on Wall Street with unregulated derivatives, shady subprime lending, and false AAA credit ratings of bundled, high-risk mortgages were the unspoken norm for those involved. The resulting global financial crash of 2008 and the trillions of dollars of economic damage led to few, if any, mea culpas or apologies. An untroubled or disowned conscience, however, does not protect anyone or their descendants from the consequences of their actions. When harm has been done, some form of atonement may show up in the family system years later. Often the person atoning for the wrongdoing may have no conscious understanding that he or she has taken on this role. When this happens that person is entangled with the actions and fate of others. Fortunately, a constellation can bring to awareness the nature of the entanglement and the measures that will facilitate its release.

*Blind Loyalty:* Whereas tribal loyalty is about group affiliation, blind loyalty is more orientated toward someone in the family system. Somehow a person can unconsciously take on or reenact the difficult fate of another family member. There is no rational reason to do so. Losing one's job won't help anyone else in the family who lost his job. This replication may be an act of misguided loyalty or love but it is still misguided. The way out is to have someone represent the afflicted family member in a constellation. The loyal person should honor the fate of the afflicted family member, even if the difficulty happened years in the past. It is also helpful to ask that family member to look kindly on the loyal person and give a blessing that frees the person to live his or her own life.

*The Power of Purpose:* Posing the question about purpose can be game changing. A compelling purpose has the power to inspire a divergent group of individuals to come together as a team. Without that purpose the team is at risk of devolving into a collection of individuals working at cross-purposes. The ethos of a self-organizing organization, like the Peace Corps, is that decentralization is effective when people buy in with passion and commitment to a unifying purpose. Purpose is about focusing on the client. What does success look like from the client's perspective? Too often groups get so caught up in their internal issues and concerns they forget about their clients who are their reason for being. Introducing purpose into a constellation can have a calming and organizing effect. The same is true in real life.

*The Power of Ceremony:* During my military service, I grew to appreciate the rituals and ceremonies, large and small, which were integral to this world. Change of command, hail and farewell, taps, dining in, dining out, and others were unspoken ways of affirming the bonds to one's comrades and a shared way of life. In traditional societies, community rituals such as the "monkey dance" in Bali have an overt restorative function.[6] Constellation facilitator Francesca Mason Boring relates that the traditional use of ceremony by her Cree family strengthens her practice because they *"understood the concept that ceremonies could shift the energy and change the events in someone's life for the better."*[7] Constellations share the gravitas and impact of an indigenous ceremony when the participants witness what unfolds from a place that is wordless and heartfelt.

## VUCA Worthy

There is something about a way an organization is structured and led that fosters resilience when faced with chaos. The US military uses the acronym VUCA—volatility, uncertainty, confusion, and ambiguity—to describe the characteristics of a war zone. Unit cohesion enables a military force to endure the stresses inflicted by the VUCA environment. A military veteran reviewing the "orders of the organization" detailed above would notice the similarities between the orders and the unwritten principles that define the culture of a military unit. Both of them strengthen the invisible bonds that foster alignment and cohesion within a group.

## Chapter 7
# The Sharks versus the Elephants

I t is unlikely you have seen one, but you have heard about the proverbial elephant in the room; the issues everyone knows about yet can't talk about publicly. Fostering enough safety, emotional and even physical, encourages people to open up. When the different voices in the system are heard, a mutual reality and a shared solution can be constructed. One fear that blocks this level of authenticity is that the discussion will degenerate into a gripe session. In actuality this rarely happens if management joins with staff in taking an honest look at the issues. When honesty and safety are both lacking, the regression of the group into a state of helpless frustration is more of a possibility.

The concept of the sharks in the room is basically the same idea as the elephants, with one major twist. The pain of the dysfunction is felt in the workplace but the source of that dysfunction is hidden from view. People know they have a problem, yet the nature of the problem and its cause are unclear.

An open and honest conversation might help; however, the core of the problem or issue remains because its root cause is unseen and unaddressed. Ironically, once this cause is finally articulated and put into context it does not seem so daunting. Fear has the most power when its source is felt but unseen. The leader's or facilitator's aura of calm competence gives the group confidence that they can explore, identify, and repair the source of the breakdown that troubles them.

## The Puzzle versus the Mystery

National security expert Gregory Treverton offers another lens for looking at problems. He classifies problems as either puzzles or mysteries. A puzzle can be solved if we find the right information. Plug in the missing pieces and the solution is obvious. Mysteries, on the other hand, don't have one or maybe any right answer. More information may make it harder to discern what is relevant versus what is noise. *"Mysteries require judgment and the assessment of uncertainty."*[1] Finding Osama bin Laden was a puzzle; fostering democracy in a post–Saddam Hussein Iraq was a mystery.

Change initiatives regularly founder because of these unknowns. Overconfidence and fear are both defensive mechanisms that keep groups from thinking things through at a deeper level. Understanding the hidden patterns the group is acting out helps explain the mystery they are grappling with and the way to address it. At least nine different systemic patterns or dynamics play out in the workplace. They following list examines each one.

***Perpetrator-Victim Dynamic:*** When this dynamic is imbedded in the personal and corporate psyche, it causes great distress. The boss who yells and the coworker who bullies are examples of a perpetrator who abuses others.

The employee who passively puts up with the abuse takes on the role of victim.

The source of this dynamic may be systemic, with roots that extend many years into the past. Since the source of the problem is in the past, the solution also resides there. Hellinger cautions against the tendency to indulge in judgmental righteousness; healing does not come about through retribution or condemnation, especially by a third party who assumes the role of rescuer or judge. The perpetrator and victim need to look at what occurred and grieve if healing is to take place.[2] The victim does not have the mandate or even the capacity to free the perpetrator from the consequences of his actions through forgiveness. The perpetrator has to take responsibility and accept those consequences to realize some degree of personal dignity and relief. In chapter 15 ("Professional Constellations"), the case study "The Hidden Sources of Conflict" illustrates this dynamic. It is also important to be aware that what might appear to a perpetrator-victim dynamic is actually a projection. Because someone "feels" like a victim does not mean the person or group is one. Subjective opinions are too often confused for objective facts.

**Survival Mode Dynamic:** People in survival mode feel overwhelmed by the emotions of vulnerability, fear, uncertainty, and doubt. The looming threat of layoffs could induce survival mode in an entire company. Even when job security is not an issue, the culture of some organizations seems to encourage thrashing about with rumors, back-biting, and "winner-take-all" office politics. A leader with perpetrator tendencies can easily induce survival mode feelings and behaviors in his or her staff. Surprisingly, a survival mode environment can also happen in a unit with good leadership that is well positioned for growth. The casual observer would wonder, given the absence of dire external threats, why can't everyone just get along?

If enough people in the organization unconsciously seek drama, they will find it.

When a person with a pattern for working in survival mode environments initiates a constellation, it might surface that a previous generation in the family suffered a difficult fate. During times of war and famine, the parents or grandparents may have had to survive a precarious existence in which life or death was a daily gamble. The imprint of this trauma is passed on and reenacted out of an unconscious identification or loyalty to the family system. The case study "The Fog of War" in chapter 15 shows how this dynamic unfolds.

**The Mother-Child Bond Dynamic:** How close are you to your mother? Were you held and nurtured as a child? Did you feel cherished, seen, and safe? According to Hellinger, the quality of this primary relationship determines your relationship with life.[3] The depth of your ability to open up, trust, and take in nurturing was established in your mother's arms. If the mother was not available emotionally it can impact her child's ability to fully live life, professionally and socially. The relationship was not nurturing because the flow of love from one generation to the next was somehow blocked. There is some truth in the saying that it is never too late to have a happy childhood. If the trauma in the family system is acknowledged and released it is possible to restore that natural flow of love.

Even if the mother is deceased, her grown child can take in her love on some level through a representative.

Obviously, It's overly simplistic to link professional success and a person's relationship with his or her mother. Many people who are publicly successful did not bond with their parents. If success, either public or private, seems to elude a person, however, then one of the places a systemic

facilitator would look is the quality of the mother-child relationship. Is the natural flow of love and connection there
or has something disrupted it? Has the person "taken," the
word Hellinger uses, his mother as his mother despite the
difficulties and shortcomings in their relationship? If there
is a disruption in the flow of love, then acknowledging that
loss can be a healing intervention. In the context of a family
constellation, steps taken to mitigate that disruption enable
the issue holder to reconnect with his sense of worthiness
and having a place in the world. In chapter 15, the case
study "Marketing Plan" illustrates how this dynamic can
play out in the workplace.

   ***Atonement Dynamic:*** Doing something that causes
harm to others creates an imbalance. Until balance is rees-
tablished by a compensating action, the affected system is
to some degree unstable. That instability is not limited to
the individual perpetrator's lifespan; it can also affect his or
her descendants. Unconsciously, a transgenerational drive
exists to atone or compensate in some way for what was
done.[4] For one businessman, this issue played out in his
hiring staff who did not measure up to the demands of their
jobs. He did not intend to limit the success of his company,
but the impact was unavoidable. The case study "Staffing
Disaster" in chapter 15 explores this dynamic. Atonement
is not just for individuals. Groups can also feel burdened by
guilt and seek redemption through self-imposed suffering.
If a company has profited from unethical or illegal activities,
the personal difficulties of some employees or shareholders
could arise as another form of that unconscious atonement.

   ***Resourcefulness Dynamic:*** The ancient Greeks
and Romans believed that the hero seldom owes his success solely to his own efforts. While he may be talented
and intrepid, his victories flow from the various gods,
ancestors, and wise women who blessed him with the

wherewithal to perform heroic deeds. This principle of resource-based success is still true today. People who achieve a lot tend to have a deep bench of support to draw upon. That support is more than financial; it takes forms that are emotionally, psychologically, or spiritually based. A fundamental resource is loving parents. Mentors, mates, friends, colleagues, and teachers who saw something in you and believed in you are also significant. Other factors include education and training, previous successes, and belief systems like religion or philosophy. Many traditional societies honor their ancestors with a shrine or altar and ask for their blessings with daily prayers and offerings. Malidoma Patrice Somé, a writer and shaman from Burkina Faso, offers this thought to Westerners: *"You may not know your grandparents but they know you"*—and they will support you from the other side, especially if you remember and honor them.[5] When challenges and obstacles seem insurmountable, setting up representatives for personal and professional resources help the issue holder embody the strength and confidence needed to persevere. The case study "Gaining Confidence" in chapter 15 outlines how to renew a beneficial connection with these resources.

*Entanglement Dynamic:* Quantum mechanics uses this term to describe subatomic particles that somehow instantly reflect what is happening to each other even though there is no apparent means of communication. In systemic work there is a similar phenomenon between two people who may be related by family but are separated by time and even death. If one person is entangled in the fate of another, he is not fully living his own life, but is unconsciously acting out some incompletion in the other person's life. This dynamic show ups when a person is constantly struggling to have a successful career just like a deceased relative did.[6] Hellinger states that this identification with another is a misguided act of love. The issue holder has a subconscious desire to join a deceased loved one or to show loyalty by replicating the life of exclusion or abuse the loved one lived. Another aspect of this is the unconscious decision to suffer or die for a parent or an older sibling so they don't have to. Each person, however, is born to live his or her own life. Taking on the fate of another does not lead to a beneficial outcome. Chapter 16 ("The Search for Success"), demonstrates how this subconscious tendency can thwart a person's conscious aspirations.

**Mother's Son/Father's Daughter Dynamic:** According to Hellinger, sometimes in a family setting the mother and son will team up to form an alliance against the father. The same thing can happen with the daughter aligning with the father against the mother. These alliances have their psychological roots in the Oedipal or Electra complexes defined by Freud. The family battles for attention, affection, and control between parents and children are part of our collective psyche. They are replicated at the workplace in the issues people have with authority. It is possible the source of a woman's conflict with her female boss goes back to the conflicted relationship she had with her mother. A man's difficulties with his male boss could be rooted in his strained relationship with his father. Dr.Debra Mandel's book *Your Boss Is Not Your Mother* explores how people reenact at work the dynamics of their family of origin.[7] And even though these dynamics are best addressed through a family constellation, they often surface during a professional one.

A solution is reached when the issue holder can truly see his boss instead of a projection of his parent. The case study "The Dance between Issues" in chapter 9 ("Your Place to Stand") tells the story of a professional caught up in that form of reenactment.

***Displacement Syndrome Dynamic:*** Carl Jung observed that *"Neurosis is always a substitute for legitimate suffering."*[8] When the suffering from a trauma is too much to deal with, it gets pushed into the subconscious. Denying a troubling insecurity or the necessity of a difficult conversation has the same effect. Inevitably, not dealing with the pain creates more of it in the form of a neurosis or conflict. M. Scott Peck agrees with psychotherapist Virginia Satir that the neurotic behaviors displayed by groups or individuals are a byproduct of avoidance. As he puts it, *"A healthy organization...is not one with an absence of problems, but one that is actually and effectively addressing its problems."* [9] Many of the constellations in *Confessions of a Corporate Shaman* surfaced subconscious traumas that were the hidden source of the problems the issue holders struggled with. There is a good reason so much of this material was buried in the subconscious. Bringing it to awareness can be too painful. An underlying systemic principle is that displacement can occur across generations.[10] Even the Old Testament asserts that the "neuroses" of the fathers are visited upon the sons.[11] The challenge for the son or daughter is uncovering and facing the old pain first experienced but not fully processed in the family system by previous generations. Some of the case studies that relate to professional constellations include poignant images of this phenomena.

***Hidden Agenda/Payoff Dynamic:*** Some organizational breakdowns are difficult to fix and confusing to discuss because they provide a covert payoff. The professional or the group may believe they are doing everything possible to resolve the issue. Yet somehow it persists. Dig a bit deeper and what is revealed is that the problem is needed to keep the system in balance. The cost of solving the problem or achieving the goal is too high. An important relationship might be lost or something unwanted taken on. This dynamic shows up in a number of case studies, including "Hidden Obstacle" in chapter 15.

As much as the dynamics described above might trouble you and frustrate your ambitions, when brought to your awareness, they become your allies. If you fall into the trap of "solve the puzzle" you miss the mystery and *"follow the wrong god home."* In a puzzle the solution is external. The answer to the mystery lies within.

## Chapter 8
# Mapping the System

There are two basic formats for mapping a system. The first is using people as representatives of parts of the system. The second uses cards or other objects. With either format it is important that the question or issue explored be significant. Subjects of mild interest or passing concern are not substantive enough to warrant setting up a constellation.

When working with a management team, I usually spend time at a flip chart diagramming the issue so we can see how the different parts of the system relate to each other. When the group members work with each other, it's more likely they will raise an issue that belongs to the entire group. Non-intact or open enrollment groups are usually people who don't know or work with each other. This allows for a more informal process since just one individual, and not the group as a whole, is the issue holder. A clear, concise, and compelling goal or question will ensure that the process is robust and engaging. Clarifying the goal and its relevant parts requires skillful listening. People tend to get lost in the details of their story. If the issue holder can't state his goal in one or two sentences then, according to Hellinger, he is not ready for a constellation.[1] In a business setting, however, more discussion and analysis will usually take place. Clarifying goals and roles is frequently a necessary and time-consuming part of the process.

Ready or not, corporate clients are paying you the big bucks to help them solve their problems. You can save them and yourself considerable angst by being selective about the approach you use. A constellation might not be appropriate for a work group where trust is low and formality high. People who work together do not have the protection of anonymity. They may not be ready to discuss what the constellation might reveal. Time may be needed to build the depth of trust and understanding that will allow emotionally charged issues to be surfaced and addressed. Good judgment and a repertoire of different methodologies will enable you, the leader or facilitator, to make the right call.

## The Systemic Taxonomy

The details people share about their challenges are different for each person. The underlying structure behind those details, however, is similar. If they have a problem, they are looking for a solution. If they have a question, they are looking for an answer. The solution and the problem are embedded together in the same system. Creating distinctions enables you to separate out and embody the different parts of that system so the solution can be seen. The taxonomy for those distinctions helps you manage the flow of the constellation. This taxonomy has six parts.

***The Issue Holder:*** This term is interchangeable with the client, the focus, or the person who has an issue that will be explored systemically. Guided by the facilitator the issue holder picks and arranges the representatives for his or her constellation. Even though the constellation is conducted for the benefit of the issue holder, the representatives often find that they gain in some meaningful way from their participation. Management constellations differ from other constellation formats in that the intact group itself can be the issue holder.

**The Representative:** This term refers to the person or item selected to represent a part of the system. This part could be a person (your boss), a group (the marketing department), a concept (like morale), or even an aspect of the company infrastructure (the IT system). In the initial setup, the issue holder arranges the representatives spatially in a way that reflects their current relationship to each other. The job of the representative is to notice what he or she notices. Acting out any type of behavior based on expectations or assumptions should be avoided. Just noticing allows the subconscious to access the knowing field. According to Einstein, *"The separation between me and you is an illusion of the conscious mind."* Accessing the subconscious mind connects us to a deeper truth that we all share.

**The Issue:** The question or problem being explored is also known as the issue. Defining the question or problem succinctly ensures a more robust and meaningful outcome. Questions that are merely an exercise in curiosity should be avoided. If the issue holder has some "skin in the game" then the constellation is more likely to produce compelling insights. It is essential that the issue holder be clear about the issue and committed to doing something about it. When people cannot sum up what they want in one or two sentences it indicates they may not be ready for a constellation. In his book *Ritual*, Malidoma Patrice Somé makes a similar point: namely, that purpose is the driving force of healing rituals in an indigenous community. If the ritual lacks a purpose it could turn against those who perform it.

*What Is:* As the dynamic between the representatives unfolds, the facilitator checks back with the issue holder to see if the reality being presented matches her perceptions of how things are. Frequently the issue holder will say, "That's exactly how it is." Just the act of establishing and affirming "what is" is an intervention that can lead to an internal shift.

*The Source:* The problem being constellated is usually symptomatic of a deeper dynamic that has roots in the past. The current dysfunction might subconsciously represent a traumatic event or traumatized person that is still affecting current reality. Identifying the person and the trauma takes the impact from the unconscious to the conscious level where it can be addressed.

*The Resolution:* In resolving the problem, the representatives speak words or phrases to affirm what is and harmonize the relationship between them. The facilitator usually provides the words based on his or her sense of what needs to happen. Not infrequently, a representative will be inspired to speak or make gestures that offer insight or bring a sense of resolution. The facilitator manages the flow of comments or movements to assure that they are authentic and not an effort to force a predetermined outcome.

## Placing the Representatives

During the initial discussion I listen closely to the issue holder and observe the person's body language. Once I have an inner image about the issue I ask the issue holder to pick representatives for specific parts of the system. Along with people, things, or ideas it is not unusual for the individual to ask to have a country or an abstract concept like purpose or trust represented.

In this same conversation with the issue holder, I am on the lookout for a felt-sense that indicates we are ready to set up the representatives. You may recall that the representative is a volunteer who holds the space for a part of the system. The part could be another person, a group, a function, or an idea. This sense of readiness comes to me somatically instead of mentally. If I don't have it, I keep interacting with the issue holder. Something has to click at the finer level of feeling and body awareness. When it does, that is my go-ahead.

After the representatives are identified I ask the issue holder to find the right place for each one in an open space. If it is just the two of us I might ask her to place cards on the floor or a table to represent the parts of the system. If the representatives are open to it, it is best if the issue holder gently guides them by their shoulders or hands to their initial spot. I usually ask the representatives to stand with their hands by their sides and simply "notice what they notice." There is no need to be or do anything except trust the feelings and thoughts that arise within. No acting is required, and the less the representatives think about the details provided by issue holder the better. The tendency of the rational mind to complicate things with long explanations should be avoided. The systemic process is not rational or conceptual. What rings true is simple, unadorned, and unanticipated. Issues remain convoluted and opaque when the analytical mind is overused.

After half a minute or so, I check in with the representatives. What do they notice? It may be a sensation, an emotion, a thought, or all three. Their feedback is then confirmed with the issue holder who will often exclaim how accurately what was said reflects the actual situation. At the appropriate time, as the facilitator, I may do the following:

**1.** Invite the initial representatives to follow any
impulse they have to move.
**2.** Select and place other representatives.
**3.** Give words or phrases to them to speak.
**4.** Assess the impact of those words on the speaker
and others.

Each of these steps is testing my hypothesis to see
if it has a restorative effect. Words and movements may
come to the representatives or I might provide them. What
is revealed comes without preconceptions. The source is
beyond the conscious, thinking mind. Allowing, trusting,
and being open and present in the moment maintains the
connection to that source which has many names, including the knowing field.

**The Solution**
The effect of the spoken words or movements can
be seen in the faces and body language of the representatives. If they have a good effect something at the collective
level shifts. The representatives relax or look lighter. The
tone of their interactions or their mood as a group changes.
As Hellinger bluntly puts it, *"If there's no relief, you haven't
found the solution, regardless of what your theory tells
you."* If the solution is found, *"all of those in the system feel
whole and at peace."*[2] As the good solution starts to unfold,
the issue holder is invited to take his place in the constellation and to absorb what the resolution to his issue looks
and feels like. Alternatively, he may have a better perspective staying outside the constellation. Seeing a resolution
unfold where none seemed possible creates a shift—not
just mentally, but emotionally, physically, and spiritually
as well. I suspect this multidimensionality creates new

pathways between the neurons in the brain that thinking alone can't do. The subconscious mind utilizes those new pathways and the images they form. Over time it inspires the conscious mind to adapt the attitudes and actions that lead to a more beneficent reality.

A guiding principle in this work is being solution focused. Once the goal is identified then the question to ask is simply what measures will mitigate the obstacles? What resources will strengthen the issue holder and enable him to achieve his goal? Paradoxically, the facilitator does not engage with a healing agenda. According to Judith Hemming, a well-known constellation facilitator from Great Britain, *"Holding an intention to 'discern the truth' is going to serve our clients much more than any intent to 'heal,' to 'solve,' to 'fix,' or to 'do' anything 'for' our clients."* [3] Hellinger affirms that the facilitator *"renounces all personal aims and intentions...letting go of any intention to control the results...remaining collected in the empty void [of the knowing field]...allowing herself to be guided by it step by step...she voices what comes to her without the expectation that it is the absolute truth."* [4]

It can happen during a professional constellation that the issue holder is deeply touched by the experience even when the obvious signs of tears, sighs, or wide eyes are not evident. Whether emotions arise or not, it's best to sit with the experience for a period of time to digest and integrate it before discussing it with others. If the group needs to debrief what they experienced I might ask the issue holder to take a break outside the room. Right after a constellation can be a tender time and the questions or comments of others may feel intrusive.[5] This is less likely to be the case with a management or an organizational constellation since the issues explored tend to be more objective and less personal in nature.

### Systemic Levels One and Two

One fascinating aspect of the constellation process is that you never know where you and the issue holder might end up, even when you start off with what seems to be a fairly innocuous question or concern. What Hellinger talks about as a sense of relief or well-being is the outcome of some shift in cognition that is more than a mental thought. That "more than" represents a cognitive or neurological shift that could be called "level two" work. You observed and interacted with the system, and that observation and interaction led to a felt-sense that touched you at the level of your being. If you had stayed only in the prefrontal cortex—the place of language and linear thinking—you would have had insights, but as a mental exercise. That type of knowing could be called "level one" work. It's what happens when you read a book or hear a lecture. You might gain a lot of information about leadership, for example, but that does not mean your employees or colleagues will notice any new leadership behaviors. Talking a good game is easy; living that game, however, requires more than intellectual knowledge.

A level two experience means the brain's neurons somewhere in the nonverbal part of the limbic system have been rewired and a new set of behaviors is now possible. If we walked out of the room feeling different than when we walked in, the session reached level two. You can sense this in how the participants relate to each other. Level two is almost a given when the issues being explored are ones which the issue holders are fully committed to resolving. In level two work, a link is uncovered between some aspect of the symptom and a traumatic event—or a traumatized person or group—buried in the past. Bringing to awareness this disowned or forgotten part sometimes unleashes considerable energy and emotion that was unknowingly repressed. You could not have anticipated what you found. The unanticipated and spontaneous nature of how things unfold touches the issue holders at their core.

A level one constellation can still be considered successful. The mandate in an organizational constellation is sometimes limited to taking a look at the system. The participants are not affected emotionally by what they see and don't need to be. They are neither seeking nor aware of the possibility for the deeper changes instigated by level two work. Success is getting exposed to the different voices within the system like those in the case study "ISO World Class Status" in chapter 12 ("Management Constellations"). Hearing those voices and their concerns and working on a set of measures to address them is a major step forward toward that status.

## The Disclaimer

It rarely occurs when a skilled facilitator is involved, yet there are occasions when the issue holder leaves a constellation confused, unhappy, or unconvinced about the outcome. I tell participants they are the arbitrators of what works for them. They don't have to accept their constellation as applicable, valid, or the final word. It is possible the representatives were not clear and got caught up in their own issues. The facilitator could have misinterpreted the dynamics she observed. The constellation may have uncovered one aspect of the issue, yet other aspects needed to be addressed before a sense of resolution could be gained. It's possible that the system was not ready to reveal a difficult secret or a forgotten trauma. The issue holder may not have been ready to confront some painful aspect of his or her past. Sometimes this shows up as a misguided effort to control the process to achieve a desired outcome. Ultimately, the one who decides what to look at or accept is the issue holder. Personal authority requires taking responsibility. Knowing when to trust one's own judgment and when to question any tendency toward self-deception is the litmus test of self-awareness. The facilitator respects this tension by inviting, but not compelling, the issue holder to look at what is behind the curtain guarding the subconscious. This invitation takes place during the pre-constellation interview and it reveals whether or not the issue holder is ready to trust the process.

# Chapter 9
# Your Place to Stand

ffective leaders know there is a place within them where they have the most access to their inner resources. This place is the balance point between two polarities: subjectivity versus objectivity, flexibility versus structure, or effort versus relaxation, to name a few. The polarities are not either/or; both are necessary. The key is to understand where you and others are in relationship to these polarities. Systems psychologist David Kantor's Four Player Model is instructive in this regard.[1] When a proposal is on the table, according to Kantor, people typically take one of four positions: someone proposes an idea (move), another person supports it (follow), and someone else either opposes it or observes what is taking place. (See Figure 9-1.) As the facilitator, where should you stand? The sweet spot is to stay in the middle of the four positions and not take sides or proclaim judgments. From this place you can ask questions and make comments that help the group understand

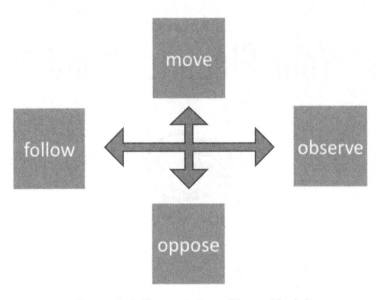

**Figure 9-1: Kantor's Four Player Model**

each other and reach a mutually agreeable solution.

This sweet spot in the above arrangement is a meta-position where observation of the four players takes place. Viewing things from an observation tower as well as the forest floor, you can assess how the parts of the system are interacting and what would bring them into harmony. However, even from a meta-position there is no completely objective observer.[2]

When you enter an organizational system as a manager, consultant, or team member, you bring your set of beliefs and bias. Seeing comes after believing. You construct your reality out of a multitude of possibilities by selecting the data that match your beliefs. If ten people, each with their own beliefs and biases, observe an emotionally charged event like a car wreck they can end up reporting ten versions of what happened. The more you discover and challenge your unconscious beliefs and the experiences they are based on, the more clarity you have as a facilitator.

Any emotional charge that affects your ability to stay neutral says more about you and your personal history than about the people and events you are reacting to.

No matter how others act or react, it is just data—or what is. Instead of wasting energy resisting or judging, keep in mind what Virginia Satir said: *"Life is not what it's supposed to be, it's what it is. The way you cope with it is what makes the difference."*[3] Satir's concept of coping with what is instead of reacting or resisting can be taken a step further according to the ancient Hawaiian practice of reconciliation and forgiveness called *"ho'oponopono."* Disharmony or conflict in others is an invitation to take full responsibility for its manifestation by owning the disharmony in oneself. The kahuna (Hawaiian for wise man or shaman) believes that clearing disharmony in oneself through prayer, apology, making amends, and ritual will bring the necessary healing to others.[4] Where the mystic perceives "oneness," the physicist "nonlocality," and the Jungian psychologist the "collective unconscious," there may be an opportunity to clear the client's field of dysfunctions, traumas, and erroneous beliefs by starting with your own.

## Déjà Vu All Over Again

It was the day before a corporate retreat and Ruth, the facilitator, had a problem. Sidra, a woman she perceived to be loud and bossy, insisted that a session covering work styles would be unethical, illegal, and disruptive to building a team. Swayed by Sidra's concerns, others were being convinced as well. Too quickly Ruth thought she was becoming one of the "them" in the "we versus them" scenario that kept the unit agitated. She felt hooked into a "no-win" situation.

Ruth recognized that giving in to a small but outspoken minority might placate them, yet accommodating them on this issue did not feel right. She telephoned a fellow facilitator, Ron, and asked him to place three cards on the floor in the room he was standing in. One was to represent her, the second for Sidra, and the third for the exercise being protested against. Ruth also laid the cards out and stood on her card. She felt like a small child facing the other two cards, unable to protect her exercise from the formidable bully who was threatening it. Feeling out of control Ruth wrote "control" on a card and placed it between the cards for Sidra and the exercise.

Ron stood on Sidra's card, and over the phone, he told Ruth it seemed to him that Sidra was feeling her voice was not heard or respected. She had offered an alternative exercise that Ruth had not accepted. Ruth was taken back to hear that someone she judged as unreasonable could be sensitive and even vulnerable. Ron placed another card on the floor for the staff of the unit and stood on it. He reported that they did not care which exercise or model was used at the retreat; they simply wanted it to be fun and productive. Ron asked Ruth where else this kind of conflict showed up in her life. She thought back to how she frequently argued with her older sibling—when they were growing up and even as adults. Ironically, both Ruth and her sibling shared the same fears of being dominated by the other. Now there was tension between them over caring for their elderly mother.

"Could you integrate Sidra's ideas into the retreat?" Ron asked. "What would you lose if you let go of some control?" Ruth confessed that she feared Sidra would dominate if she let her, taking up the "airtime" with accusations and complaints. Ron put a card titled trust in the middle of the constellation. Giving Sidra space to share her ideas was ironically about trust, something that was in short supply.

Ruth's mood shifted. Giving Sidra her due changed

how she perceived her. The mix of fear and resentment gave way to a sense of acceptance and even friendliness. Ron noted that when he represented Sidra he felt she had become friendly toward Ruth as well. Ruth wondered if her inner shift could be a precursor to a shift by the group. Could tomorrow's retreat be about strengthening and celebrating an emerging sense of community instead of rehashing the conflict over the exercise?

The next day, the dour group Ruth feared might show up figuratively stayed home. People laughed and danced in the opening icebreaker. Sidra was all smiles as she shared the three points about her relationship model. The sixty participants were pleasantly surprised by how fun and productive the retreat turned out to be. Sidra even took part in the communication exercise that had been the source of controversy. Ruth realized that taking 100 percent responsibility for any charged reaction she had toward someone like Sidra was essential. When a relationship became strained and in need of repair, the place to start was within herself. She could not expect the group to shift from fragmentation to community until she united what was fragmented within herself.

## The Dance between Issues

The following story highlights the use of self from the perspective of a change facilitator who attended one of my open enrollment workshops. As with previous examples in this and earlier chapters, Sally found her own personal change work was part of, and supported, her change work with her client. She was coaching a manager who was struggling to change the culture of her organization. Staff were angry, cynical, and disengaged. They had been that way for a long time. The leader tried everything in her sphere of power and influence to address their concerns and attitudes, but she had scant success. Sally did not want her client and the staff to give up. She hoped she could help them find new sources of strength within themselves to turn things around. The question was how to do this, and what was the best possible way?

Sally felt that the failure of her client group to stop their self-destructive ways was hers as well; a specter that demoralized her. I asked Sally to look within herself and find the places where she felt hopeless and helpless. What stopped her? What part of her resonated with this situation? In response, Sally closed her eyes. She heard the voice of her mother telling her, "Don't let your father down." Her fear of failure was twofold: first, failing, and second, disappointing her father. This message started when she was a child and her parents separated.

Representatives were chosen and placed by Sally. The voice of Sally's mother stood behind her. Her *father* sat on the floor in front of her looking up. He had had a  stroke a few years ago and could not speak. The representative for the fear of failure placed himself between them. I selected a person to represent the *spirit of her father* who could communicate with her. I asked the *spirit of her father* to reassure Sally he was proud of her no matter what.  She was doing her mission and that was victory enough.  Nothing could happen that would take her from his heart  or come before his love for her. *Fear of failure* moved away after these words were spoken. Sally told her *mother* not  to worry about Dad. He did not need Sally to hold him up. Her *father* through his spirit representative blessed her work and affirmed he would always be her father and she his daughter. *He* wanted her to live her own life and be  her own person. Sally embraced her *father.*

Sally's client and the staff of the organization were placed nearby. Now she could see them. She honored their fate and the choices they made. It was not her role to save them from life's disappointments nor could they save her or her father from theirs. They smiled at her and she smiled back. She would help those who were ready to be helped, and that renewed her sense of purpose and confidence. Sally left the workshop in a more resourceful and confident state.

When a mistaken belief is cleared up, sources of energy and power are more available. People may not be aware of their erroneous beliefs, but they usually are acutely aware of the difficulties that result. Surfacing those subconscious beliefs and correcting them with affirming ones is like imbibing a restorative and empowering tonic.

# PART II

# Raising Organizational IQ

*It's not enough to have smart people in your organization. Your organization also needs to be smart. A dumb organization makes everyone in it seem less smart. Dysfunctions in people, systems, or outputs are symptoms of this dumbing down. Corrective actions that don't address the sources of those dysfunctions foster cynicism or apathy. The hidden dynamics explored in the following case studies inhibited the ability of the organizations to learn, share information, and adapt. Dysfunctions, like silos or we-versus-they rivalries, indicate a lack of collective intelligence imposed by hidden obstacles. Smart organizations find answers to urgent problems, be it a mystery or a puzzle, because of how they work as a system. Malcolm Gladwell recounts in* What the Dog Saw and Other Adventures *that at the start of WWII, America's merchant marine was badly mauled by German U-boats while the British managed to defend their shipping.[1] The British had an organizational system that strategically coordinated their naval activities. Not until the Tenth Fleet was formed to harmonize their fragmented antisubmarine warfare efforts did the United States Navy achieve similar results. Addressing a critical problem from a more systemic perspective enhances the capacity to make connections between seemingly unrelated pieces of information and take prescient actions.*

## Chapter 10

# Organizational Constellations

The majority of the workplace issues outlined in this chapter were constellated at open enrollment workshops. In each exploration, the orders of organizations were used to unpack the systemic issues that lay behind the overt problem. Once the issue was identified and the dynamic between its component parts observed, tentative solutions were then introduced and tested.

## Cultural Innovation

New facilitators will notice it is a fairly straightforward endeavor to set up an accurate picture of a situation using representatives. The initial placement of the representatives will reflect the "stuckness" felt in the real situation. Now what? If the next steps toward resolution had been obvious the issue holder would have taken them already. Drawing upon the orders of organizations, the skilled facilitator will come up with a hypothesis and then test it. One type of test is to put in a representative that could be the source of the stakeholder's issue. Not announcing who or what is being represented allows for a more objective test of that hypothesis. If the new representative was named, it is possible that the other representatives might respond mentally instead of with their felt-sense. These techniques were used with the following constellation.

Fran had recently been hired by an American manufacturing firm to help change the culture of the company. The firm wanted to foster a culture that encouraged innovation for its 12,000 employees. Fran had worked with the firm in the past and knew that previous initiatives had gone nowhere. She took the job but was not confident that the outcome in this latest initiative would be any different. Noticing her lack of enthusiasm, I asked her if the "change fairy" happened to come along next week and bopped everyone there on the head with a change wand, what would be different? Besides seeing more innovation what else would have changed?

One potential change, Fran responded, was that employees would be more willing to take risks because top management was backing them up and not punishing failure. There would be more trust and less guardedness around the pervasive fear of losing one's job in uncertain economic times. Okay, but how could Fran be successful if people regarded the change process as a ticket to be punched rather than an essential password to success?

Given what she had to work with, where and how in the system could she intervene? Fran chose representatives for the *senior management team,* the *sponsor* of the initiative, and the *change team* leading the new initiative and set them up in the arrangement shown in Figure 10-1. The representative for the *change team* reported that they did not feel engaged in the project. The main goal was to stay

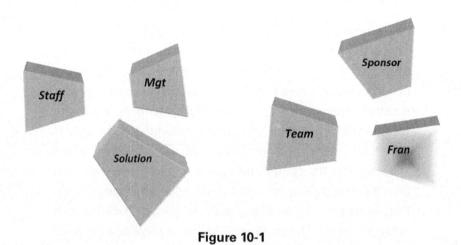

**Figure 10-1**

employed and not rock the boat. The sponsor, who reported to the VP of HR, did not have much of a connection with the *change team* or *senior management*. He was hopeful Fran could make wonderful things happen which would make him look good. *Senior management* was a little uneasy at first with what the people behind him might be up to, but he did start feeling he could rely on the sponsor to keep things in control and avoid negative surprises.

A representative for the 12,000 employees was added. She did not feel a part of the change process and just wanted to know what was expected of her. The situation seemed stuck. Something was needed to move things forward, but what? Another representative was added without her role being announced. She found her place beside company staff. She reported feeling very grounded and rooted as if her feet were filled with a warm energy that needed to be expressed. She also felt very connected to the staff. I told the group this representative was the solution. No real progress could be expected without involving the firm's employees. Still, *senior management* was not really paying much attention to the change initiative, and the *sponsor* did not want their attention. The *change team* was open to action as long as it wasn't risky.

A representative was added as the part of the culture that somehow sustained the status quo. There was no movement. Something else was still needed. I put in another representative without saying who or what she was. "What happened when she entered the space?" I asked. The other representatives noticed it felt best when she was near the center and visible to all. This new person was the compelling reason for change (see Figure 10-2). People had to realize they could no longer "kick the can down the road." The arrangement gave everyone a sense of hope, and the *status quo* slowly withdrew from the center of the circle. *Staff* still wanted to know how the change was going to take place and their role in making it happen. The *change team* handed them a notebook that represented the plan, but this gesture was not convincing. The *sponsor* then took the plan from the *change team* and handed it to *senior management,* who then handed it to the *staff.* The constellation indicated the need for a visible and compelling purpose for change. Everyone might not buy in, but a well-crafted and communicated rationale would bring enough people onboard.

Senior management's endorsement of the plan and their commitment to it was a vital part of this outreach. Fran left with the sense that she had a way forward. She now felt hopeful about the project and her capacity to make a difference.

### International Ping Pong

Pam, the US manager for an international development organization, was feeling anxious about a large project she supervised in a developing country. The project had seen significant turnover, including its third chief of party in two years. The donors had been on the verge of eliminating

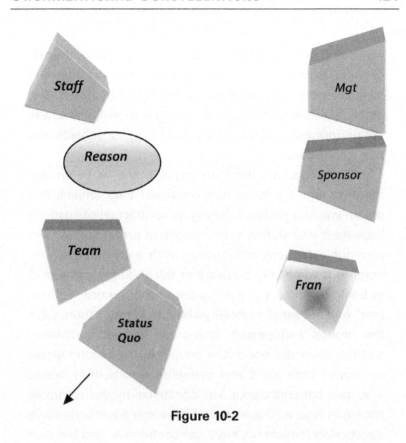

**Figure 10-2**

funding because of their assessment of its poor performance, which included the low quality of deliverables. The newly hired chief had Pam's full confidence, yet the intense pressure to turn the project around had begun to negatively impact his health. Pam felt that the project would not succeed until the entire project team learned how to work together more collaboratively. Some of the lack of communication and coordination might stem from personality conflicts, but professional skills were also a significant concern. Although there were a number of competent staff, some members of the project were still struggling to master the technical aspects of their jobs. Local labor laws made it cost prohibitive to fire anyone. The thin labor market meant qualified professionals were difficult to find. The new chief was doing the right things: meeting one-on-one with staff, defining expectations, strengthening accountability, and taking steps to enhance the capacity of individual staff. One of the key staff, who had crosscutting responsibilities, was not performing, and the solution of hiring consultants was being considered.

What outcome did Pam desire if she woke up one morning and a miracle had occurred? Pam smiled. Her dream was the project fulfilling its contractual obligations because it was staffed with competent professionals who communicated and collaborated with each other. I wondered if it was really accurate or fair to judge some staff as being competent and some not since the word "competent" had the sense of finality about it. Perhaps there were two groups, I suggested. One group had her confidence and the other did not. If the people in the second group developed their skills and delivered results, they would also gain her confidence. The constellation was set up as shown in Figure 10-3: staff that have management's *confidence,* staff that *do not* have her confidence, and the contractual *obligations* the project must fulfill to be successful.

Confidence

Obligations

No Confidence

**Figure 10-3**

Both *staffs* felt isolated and uncertain about their roles and their relationship to the contractual obligations. *Obligations* felt alone. The representatives were asked to move as they felt inspired. The two *staffs* moved closer to each other and to the *obligations,* as depicted in Figure 10-4. *Obligations* turned away from the *staffs,* especially the *no confidence staff.*

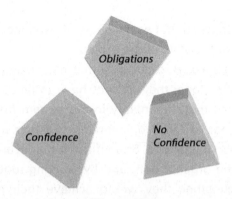

**Figure 10-4**

The movements did not alleviate the tension for the *staffs;* both still felt anxiety over their roles and places. "It's like things are ping-ponging around," stated the *confidence staff.* A representative for that anxiety was added to the constellation. This allowed *obligations* to turn and face the *staffs.* Both *staffs,* especially the *confidence staff,* felt better.

I asked Pam to take her place in the constellation. She noted she was very anxious about the situation. (See Figure 10-5.) A representative for her anxiety was added to

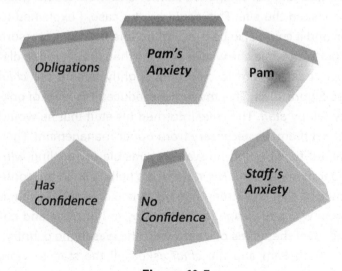

**Figure 10-5**

distinguish between her as the US-based manager and her anxiety about the state of the project.

Pam was asked to tell *staff* that her anxiety was her responsibility, alone; they did not have to take it on. She acknowledged that the anxiety in the system made it difficult for them to focus on working together to achieve their contract obligations. She affirmed that everyone had a place in the organization, and by working together and helping each other, they would achieve their goal. This message helped calm *staff* down and alleviate their anxiety. Pam further stated that she was getting ready to travel to the field office for a site visit. In anticipation of that visit, a representative was chosen for the chief who was the project leader based in the country. The *chief* and Pam moved to where they both could better see *obligations* and their *staff*. But, this move raised the anxiety of the *confidence* staff directly facing Pam, *whose representative* reported that she felt like crying.

Pam was a bit chagrined and stated that the project staff had told her things felt calmer and more stable when she visited the site. This could be the case, I explained to her, and it could also be true that people felt more pressure to perform while she was in-country than they cared to disclose. I asked Pam to step back slightly behind the *chief* (see Figure 10-6). This movement reduced the level of anxiety felt by *staff*. The *chief* informed his staff that he would protect them  as necessary from upper management. They worked for him and he was responsible for dealing with upper management. *His* statements helped build the confidence of *staff* and strengthen the sense of order. This interaction was a message to Pam to stay in her place and not take  over the duties of chief when she was in the country.

Both Pam and the *chief* asked all the staff to work together to strengthen their professional capacity and

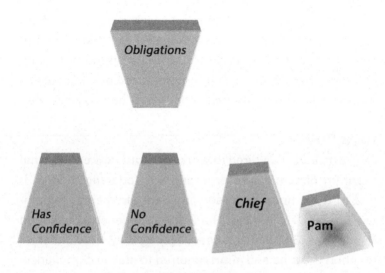

**Figure 10-6**

fulfill the contract obligations. *Staff* pointed out that the bigger vision about the positive impact the project could have in improving health and reducing mortality should be communicated frequently by management. The closing movements and statements seemed to bring the project team to a place of optimism and alignment.

**Reflections:** Pam, the manager at headquarters, was able to see from the constellation how her anxiety and actions could adversely impact the confidence and sense of order of the project staff in the field. She had to balance supporting the chain of command with the urgent need to see results. Too much intervention on her part could undermine the role of the project chief, which in turn would undermine the possibility of a turnaround. Yet, the donors only had so much patience. Clearly the chief was on the right track. Building up internal capacity through coaching was a long-term solution. Augmenting capacity by hiring consultants and/or the reassignment of key staff were two solutions that could be implemented more quickly. Hopefully, Pam could buy the chief the time he needed with the donors to take corrective action and help him line up the necessary resources. This approach would optimize both her role as the manager and the limited options they had to work with.

## Hard Start

Bob had been hired to work with four new educational program directors. The program was federally funded. It had to meet numerous regulatory requirements to maintain funding. The directors had little experience with federal regulations. Bob had an uneasy feeling they were underestimating the time and effort required to stay in compliance. His job was to help them develop a collaborative partnership and meet the obligatory regulations. He was feeling anxious about their ability to adapt to a bureaucratic environment and the impact that might have on their desire and ability to collaborate with him and each other. What could he do that would enhance the possibility of success?

Four representatives were chosen to be the directors and one to represent the federal regulations. I asked Bob to set up the *regulations* and the four *directors,* then to sit and observe while I asked each representative in turn what they noticed. The *first director* felt confident as he faced the *regulations.* The *others, however,* each in turn felt increasingly uncomfortable with the situation. The *fourth director* felt isolated from the others and uncomfortable facing the *regulations.*

Bob nodded in agreement as they reported in turn. A representative for himself was chosen and asked to go find his place. Bob wandered over to the side of the *regulations* and stood there facing the *directors* (see Figure 10-7). The regulations felt uneasy having Bob standing there. The directors were not reassured either. Bob was then asked to take his place in the constellation. His representative stood

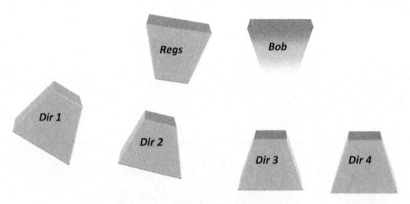

**Figure 10-7**

behind him as his inner resource of experience and wisdom. What should he say or do to help resolve the situation? He didn't know and appeared to be stuck. An appeal to work together to meet the regulations did little to close the awkward gap between the two groups. I then placed a new representative where both groups could see her. I had Bob tell the directors, "This is your purpose as an organization. One that is meaningful and motivating to everyone here." The *directors* moved closer and after some milling around sorted themselves out around the *purpose* and Bob. An open space indicated someone else might be needed on the team.

After some discussion it was apparent that Bob had three jobs. One was helping the directors define their common purpose and unite around it. The second one was helping them build the collaborative structures they would need to deliver services to their clients. His third role, keeping the group in compliance with the federal regulations, was in conflict with the first two. Bob was either the compliance cop or a trusted partner, but not both. Someone else was needed to be the technical person who could explain the regulations. It so happened that there was someone Bob knew who could take on that role, as shown in Figure 10-8.

When *regulations* took her place in the new

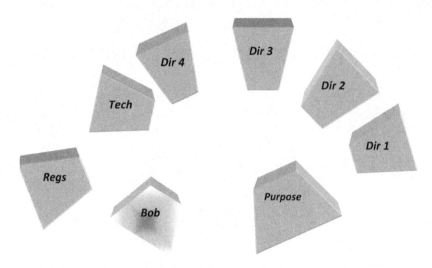

**Figure 10-8**

structure that was being formed, *everyone* but her felt better. *Regulations* felt too much attention was being paid to *her alone.* She stepped back behind Bob and the *technical person.* A gap was left where she could see and be seen. One of the observers who was familiar with the situation pointed out that the constellation now represented perfectly how the organization's focus was skewed toward the federal regulations instead of the clients it served. Recently, she had been at a conference where no one mentioned the organization's purpose once during several days of meetings. All their discussions and presentations had been about compliance.

I asked Bob to step back out of the constellation and take in from an expanded vantage point the desired outcome of his work. How did that feel in his body? Bob reported that his anxiety had been replaced by a sense of confidence and excitement about what he and his clients could achieve. An insight he gained was the centrality of the organization's purpose and the clients it served. If the regulations always had center stage it would lead to needless conflict and a loss of focus among his working group.

**Reflections**: Bob reported back to me by email a few weeks later. *"The experience was very powerful and affected all subsequent work. I stressed our common goal in all my conversations with other consultants and with the directors of the partner agencies. This proved to help us move closer in our relationship. The exercise changed my whole approach to the situation and to my work!"*

## Cross-Sector Change Management

An organization with an individualistic culture wanted to move to a more collaborative approach in working with clients and partners. The director of the unit expected staff to voice their resistance to this new approach. The transaction cost—basically time and effort—would be high initially. His professionals, who were independent dealmakers, tended to work on their own. Involving them in a team approach would take away some of the independence they cherished, even though in the longer run it would pay off in more profitable project outcomes.

An internal change management specialist, Sita was joining the department to move the change process forward. During a management training program, she asked for coaching on how to meet the challenges of her new job. She agreed to try the constellation process so we selected representatives for the different parts of the system. These were: the new change specialist (Sita), the director (dir), investment professionals (IPs), the new strategy of collaboration (strategy), and its successful results (result). The new strategy was represented by a piece of paper that was placed on the floor. Sita arranged the representatives as shown in Figure 10-9.

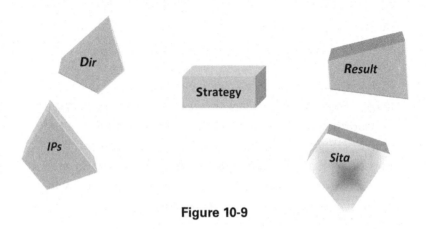

**Figure 10-9**

The representatives were asked to report what they noticed or felt while they stood in this arrangement.

Sita confirmed that the initial impressions they offered were accurate. The *investment professionals (IPs),* standing at a distance and facing away from the others, were happy to be focused on their own world. They did not care to be bothered with things that took time away from negotiating deals with their clients. Sita was feeling anxious about how she was going to involve the IPs and their reaction to her overtures. The director was focused on the new strategy and supportive of Sita, he but expected her to know what to do.

The *results* were looking to the *strategy* but felt disconnected from the others. The *director's* impulse was to go to the *IPs* and drag them forcefully over to the strategy so they would do what he said. I allowed *him* to go to the *IPs,* but not to force them to move physically. The *IPs* reluctantly faced the director. The *director* told the *IPs* that he was their boss and they would be evaluated on their support for the new strategy. The *IPs* moved a few feet toward to the new *strategy,* but their attention was still directed toward how they used to do business. Sita, in response to the stalemate, moved halfway to a place next to the *IPs* and the *director,* but not too far away from the new strategy. The *IPs* confessed they would rather not be bothered. Sita pointed to the *result* standing near the new *strategy.* By aligning with the *strategy* they would achieve a new level of results. *"Please see the link between the two,"* she requested the *IPs.* The *IPs* felt motivated to move toward the better *result,* but they still regarded the *strategy* as an afterthought. The representatives experimented with finding what felt best and came up with the order shown in Figure 10-10.

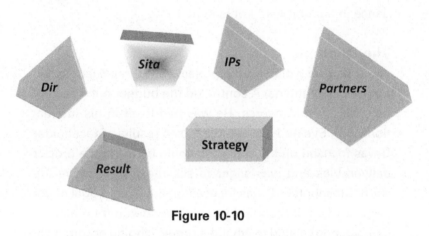

Dir

Sita

IPs

Partners

Strategy

Result

**Figure 10-10**

The group arranged itself around the new *strategy,* yet something was missing. A representative was chosen for the partners who would be engaged with the new strategy and given a place in the constellation. They felt they were beginning to come together and would keep moving in the direction, given sufficient communication and leadership.

**Reflections:** As a newcomer, Sita had to establish her role as the bridge between the strategic vision of the director and the concerns of the IPs. Several factors for a successful change process emerged during the constellation: (1) Sita should develop her relationship with her boss and ask for his support in motivating the IPs; (2) The director might force compliance from the IPs, but their commitment would still be doubtful. Asking for their understanding and cooperation and applauding small victories would help win that commitment; (3) Sita had to make the case that everyone would benefit from the new strategy; and (4) If Sita could involve the IPs and partners directly in the change process and build coalitions with them, she would demonstrate her bona fides as a "go-getter." Sita left the session with a plan to establish her place in the unit and to inspire more confidence in her ability to implement it.

### The Dilemma

Eve was working on a project with three client stakeholders. Stakeholder A controlled the budget but was very political and risk averse. He was hands-off in his interactions with Eve and just wanted to see results. Stakeholder B was focused on the staff that would be using the project deliverables and was eager to see the project move forward. Stakeholder C was focused on the overall goal of the project. Eve felt blocked by C and wondered if he had his own agenda related to what the project should accomplish. Eve was nervous about her role and its duration. Her participation in the project would not be settled for another month. How could she position herself for the best outcome? What dynamics, hidden or not, did she need to pay attention to during this period of uncertainty?

Eve set up the initial constellation as shown in Figure 10-11. Eve's representative reported feeling unstable. She swayed back and forth toward one stakeholder then another, pulled or pushed by their differing expectations. Given the direction the *stakeholders* were facing, the unacknowledged tension between *stakeholders B* and *C*, the unwillingness of *stakeholder A* to take any initiative,

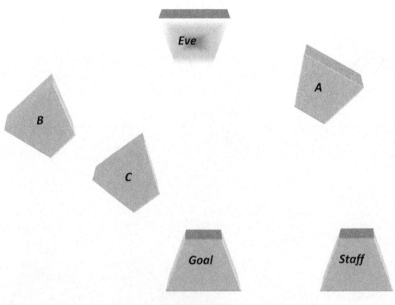

**Figure 10-11**

along with the holding pattern Eve had been consigned to, it seemed unlikely that the group would take the risk to engage in a difficult but potentially productive conversation. When a representative for the staff who would be served by the project was placed in the constellation, the dynamic in the group immediately changed. Everyone looked at the *staff* with a sense of purpose and expectancy. *Staff* appreciated the attention and were content to be the object of their focus. The stakeholders liked the shift to focusing on *staff,* but they felt somewhat frustrated with their progress. They seemed stuck in the same configuration and unable to talk to each other about how to move forward. This logjam was dissolved when Eve moved closer to staff. From her new position she would see all the stakeholders from their perspective. *Stakeholder C* moved over to the goal and faced the group. The moves resulted in the configuration in Figure 10-12.

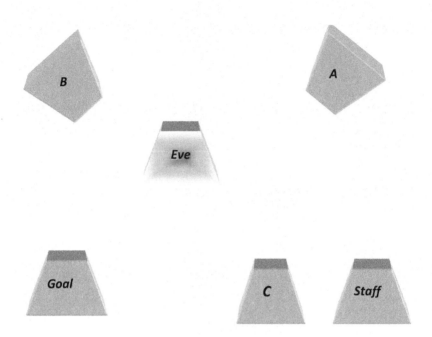

**Figure 10-12**

From the perspective of the goal, *stakeholder C* could keep track of the results of the project and how it impacted the big picture. *Stakeholder B* stayed where she was and continued to focus on *staff*. She was happy to see that they were being served by Eve. *Stakeholder A* liked it that both the organizational goal and the staff were being attended to. Eve and the *stakeholders* each had their place where they were better positioned to communicate with each other and attend to the project in the areas where they felt most involved.

**Reflections:** Eve had two choices. She could stay on the sidelines and wait for others to decide her fate, or she could take action and include herself. The Jesuits have a saying that it is better to ask for forgiveness than permission. Since she had a natural mandate as the go-between for the stakeholders and the staff, the Jesuits' approach appeared to be the way to go. Soliciting staff input and aligning the purpose of the project with that input were actions that would demonstrate her place within the organization and the value she added to it.

## Musical Hot Potato

Change agents rely on formal authority and informal influence. Formal authority comes from one's place in a hierarchy and the decisions one is authorized to make. Informal influence is related to the use of self. To what extent is the speaker living the change he wishes to see in others? Words alone are not enough. People are more likely to follow the change leader when they see that her actions and way of being are congruent with her words, as the following constellation illustrates.

A new general manager had taken over a professional association. His style and expectations were different from those of the acting general manager who had held the post for over a year. The previous GM had been attuned to relationships and the well-being of staff during his tenure. The new GM was more focused on tasks. He wanted to see results and a clear demonstration of how each staff person added value. His direct reports, the office directors, were on notice that their contracts might not be renewed when they expired in six months. One of the office directors had responded by turning up the heat. Whether the work was routine or a one-off project, it all had to be completed in a hurry. Some of the projects had been dragging on for quite some time and the factors causing their slow progress seemingly had not changed. While his sense of urgency to show results was understandable, his staff felt his constant demands were fear based and unrealistic. Morale had gone down as the stress had gone up. One of the director's staff, a professional named Frieda, had experience as a management coach. She wondered if her director might be "coachable," and, if so, how she could approach him. She wanted to remind him what Ernest Hemingway meant when he said, "Never confuse movement with action."

Representatives were selected for the GM, the director, staff, and the desired results. Frieda set them up as shown in Figure 10-13.

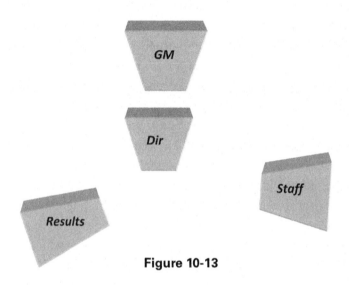

**Figure 10-13**

The *GM* felt he did not really have a sense of what was going on and was irritated that the *director* stood in his way. The *director* was ready to start making things happen. *He* seemed energized by the situation but was uneasy about what was occurring behind his back with the *GM*. The *staff* felt disengaged. *Results* was not sure about its place. The representatives were invited to follow their inclination to move, but there was little movement. Frieda was put in the constellation as her own representative. She seemed antagonistic toward the *staff* and stood at some distance from the group. What were the judgments or fears that kept her separate? Frieda only shared that the stress was creating conflicts between staff members.

I wondered about the source of this conflict. Was it related to the fear of being stuck with a "hot potato"—a project that was performing poorly and likely to remain that way? Frieda was not interested in exploring the conflict so I decided to look at another issue. I selected a representative for the purpose of the office and placed her outside the group. The group was not told who she was. The representatives were allowed to move if they felt inspired to and ended up in the arrangement shown in Figure 10-14.

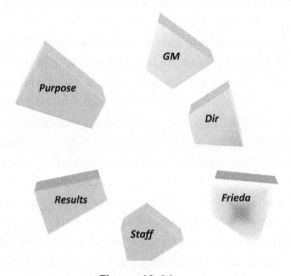

**Figure 10-14**

The group spontaneously organized themselves around the *purpose* and looked toward her as if for reassurance and inspiration. Based on this movement, I asked Frieda to tell her *director* that here was the purpose of the office. If *he* clarified the purpose to the staff and their contribution to achieving it, the results would be more likely to follow. The director followed her advice and introduced the purpose to the *staff* and the *GM*. The *director* asked his staff to work together to achieve the purpose, which united all their efforts and the results they achieved. After hearing this exchange, the GM was reassured that the office was making a difference. There was a clear sense that the office staff needed to feel that they had to sink or swim together as a team instead of jockeying individually to take the best or avoid the worst work assignments. Defining a purpose and the priorities that would support it could help persuade staff they were all in this together.

**Reflections:** It was not a surprise to see that revisiting the purpose of the unit and the teamwork behaviors needed to achieve it would help everyone deal with a challenging situation. If the reality of the office was truly a zero sum game of musical chairs then teamwork was out of the question. Each employee would have every motivation to make him- or herself look good and avoid sharing resources or advice. Yet, this approach did not energize Frieda or give her a path forward. The moment of truth was revealed in how she was distant from others in her office. Although I honored Frieda's desire not to address her strained relationships, there was scant likelihood she would be effective in helping her director pull her team together as long as she distanced herself from others. Her capacity to be a facilitator of change and a leadership coach was linked to her willingness to be self-observant and introspective.

In hindsight, I learned as a constellation facilitator to be more deliberate about if and when to put the issue holder into the constellation. It is a rare opportunity for the issue holder to see herself and her interactions with others from the place of an observer. People have an image, story, or movie they run in their heads that explains what is happening and why. A surprising amount of the time, that movie is incomplete or just plain wrong. It is too easy to overlook your part in the drama you judge others to be creating. Observing your own pattern of interactions enables you to question assumptions and tendencies so taken for granted you are hardly aware of them. Self-awareness is developed through self-observation. Perhaps if Frieda watched how her representative interacted, she would have appreciated the impact of her behaviors and been more interested in changing them.

## Survivor's Guilt

A company had been struggling from the effects of a financial downturn. The new management team decided to cut costs and lay off nearly half the staff in one of the departments. The new VP for that department was a strong personality who was clear about the direction she wanted to take. The first-level manager reporting to the VP felt marginalized by her focus on task over people. Dee, an internal leadership consultant, was working with the manager and his department to improve communication, morale, and productivity. Her question was how to optimize her impact within the system and help achieve these objectives. While Dee did not have a mandate to provide feedback to the new VP, she thought that as her relationship with the manager developed the opportunity might emerge. Representatives for the VP, the manager, the department, and Dee were selected and placed.

The sentiments expressed by each representative during an initial check-in were confirmed by the real Dee. *Staff* were feeling insecure and confused; so was the *manager*. The *VP* was focused on her goals, paying little attention to the *manager* or the *staff*. Dee wanted to help but was unsure what to do. When I stood by the *VP* I noticed something that felt like anger. Was there something in the system that was generating this dynamic? A person was selected and placed in the corner between the *VP* and *Dee* to represent the dynamic. Instead of anger, the *VP* reported pain and sadness.

What had happened to the company that could account for this sadness? I asked.

Dee mentioned again that there had been layoffs recently and half of the department had been let go. The new VP had participated in making that decision with the rest of the leadership team. A representative for those laid off was placed in the constellation. The *laid off staff* stood at a distance, facing the rest of the group (as shown in Figure 10-15). Since the layoffs had been fairly recent, it was likely that most of them had not yet found other positions. Dee was asked to take her place in the constellation and tell the *staff* and the *manager* that the layoffs were a business decision because of the economy. It was not their fault they had been let go. Dee honored the fate of laid off

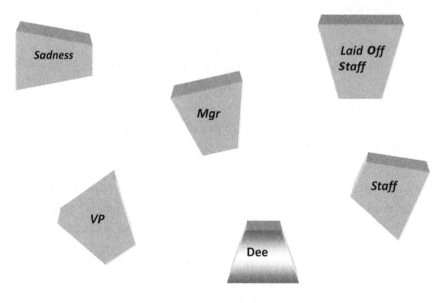

**Figure 10-15**

staff. She was sorry for what had happened, but it was necessary to keep the rest of the company afloat. The *staff* and *manager* felt better, but still uneasy. The *laid off staff* were ready to move on and go in another direction. The *VP* still seemed detached from what was happening in the unit and showed no interest in their discussions.

Dee was asked to look at the VP and say, *"I understand. You did what you had to do for the good of the company."* She admitted she had judged the VP for being unfeeling. The *VP* reported that once she felt that Dee understood her, she was ready to communicate with the group. Now *she* could explain what happened and reassure those who stayed and those who left. Paradoxically, acknowledging the trauma and sadness the layoffs had caused had a calming effect. The *staff* and *manager* felt better and more engaged after the *VP* expressed her regret for the layoffs and asked for their understanding. The *manager,* however, was still uncertain about his role relative to the *VP.* It was not Dee's job to provide that clarity, but she could encourage the manager to have a conversation with the VP about his expectations.

**Reflections:** It is not uncommon for the human impact of a business decision to be ignored by those making the decision. You may have seen Scrooge harrumph in *A Christmas Carol, "Business is not fair, it's business."* Scrooge's flaw was a willful blindness to the humanity of others. People are more than just "things." They are part of a larger system that everyone is connected to. If the sacrifice of the fired staff for the good of the whole was not acknowledged, it was likely that those who remained would suffer from survivor's guilt. Pressured by this guilt they might unconsciously feel they had to atone for what was inflicted on their colleagues. This atonement could take a number of forms, one being the failure of the business to thrive.

Dee realized that the VP needed to pay attention to people and the personal impact of her business decisions. Ironically, Dee would have more opportunity to manage up if she was more active in managing her own judgments. As an internal leadership coach she had a mandate to enhance the leadership effectiveness in her organization at any level that was receptive. That receptivity, in turn, would be greater if she could find the place of non-judgment within herself.

## Change Starts with the Changer

A manager in the public sector had a tough year. A number of employees in her department were dealing with the death or serious illness of close family members. Previously the department had run like clockwork, but these deaths and illnesses had taken their toll. An older woman, well liked and respected, had been the catalyst in bringing the employees together, but she had retired. A new staff member, Les, was transferred from another department to fill her position. He had an accident soon after he arrived and was out for several months. When he returned he could not be relied upon and disappeared for long periods of time without any communication. Though Les had a long history of substandard performance before he was assigned, he acted shocked and defensive when counseled about his behavior. HR and senior management were reluctant to support any disciplinary action because of the potential for charges of discrimination. Morale was low in the department in part because of this lack of accountability and extra work forced upon the other employees.

The manager hoped to turn the situation around. She knew her chances of reforming her wayward staff member were slim, but nonetheless, she hoped a team-building session with the entire group might make a difference. During our exploratory discussion in her office she used seven small plastic figures to map the relationships between her team members (arranged as shown in Figure 10-16).

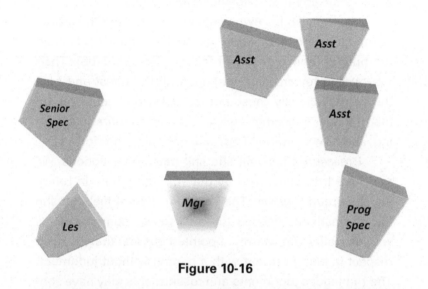

**Figure 10-16**

The figure for *Les,* not surprisingly, was looking away from the group. *The program specialist* and the *senior specialist* were also off in their own worlds. The three *adjunct staff assistants,* part-time employees, were looking to the *manager or the program specialist* for direction, although normally they should be looking to the senior specialist.

I asked the manager to verbalize why her department was so fragmented. The figures seemed locked up in their own worlds. What was keeping them there? Even though no staff were in the room to speak their thoughts, the manager felt that she had a new insight. They all had a private grief or trauma they were still mourning. Their supportive "grandmother," who would have helped them acknowledge and work through their grief, had been replaced by a person who would not or could not do his fair share. As long as Les could not be held accountable, I told her, it would not be possible to have a team. A team-building event was unlikely to be successful because Les would almost certainly not show up. If he did, he would likely leave as soon as the topic about his behavior was raised.

Ironically, in his own way, Les was serving the group. Complaining to each other about Les, they could shift the bulk of their unresolved feelings into his inbox. Their resentment toward him contained all the angst and pain they unconsciously chose not to deal with. I could see on the manager's face her disappointment that first counseling, and now team-building, was not going to reform Les.

I reassured her that she still had some options. We reviewed the role played by the "grandmother" in bringing the group together. The manager did not feel that she had the patience needed to listen to someone's troubles with empathy and warmth. I pointed out that there is deep respect in being present with a person without judgment. The manager's judgments and resentments may have contributed to the negative hallway chatter. If anything was going to change, it would have to start with her attitude and how she saw the situation. First in her mind, and then in practice, she could recognize each team member and the pain they were facing in their personal lives. In our discussion she appreciated her staff's dedication in showing up and doing the best they knew how under difficult circumstances. To Les, she acknowledged his unconscious service to the group in carrying its collective and unspoken pain, and the resentment and anger that pain gave rise to. She affirmed that this role of a scapegoat was no longer needed nor desired. Each person must take responsibility for his or her own emotions. Les's role henceforth would be to simply do the work assigned to him according to his place in the hierarchy.

After affirming a new attitude of personal responsibility,

the manager reorganized the figures, putting each team member in place. She included the purpose of the unit which would serve as their focal point. (Figure 10-17 shows the manager's new arrangement of her department.)

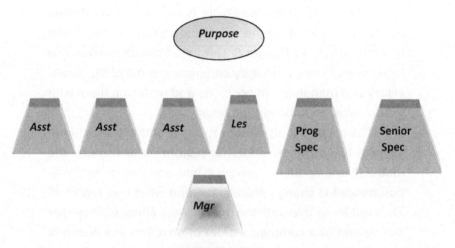

**Figure 10-17**

**Reflections:** Six months later I ran into the manager in one of the hallways of the headquarters building. She confided that there had been emotional meetings, but progress had been made in turning around the wayward member and the morale of the group. Changing her own attitude so she could see Les in a new light had been the essential step toward achieving the changes she wanted.

## Organizational Evolution

A midsize company was getting a lot of publicity for embracing a manager-less structure called Holacracy. Its transition, according to media reports, had been bold in scope but not seamless in execution. The question explored by a constellation practice group I belonged to was this: *How should this company manage the change to Holacracy to ensure that it obtains the desired results?*

If the new structure proved successful it was likely that other companies would follow, seeking the potential benefits of a more productive and innovative workforce. The idea that employees should make the decisions that are at their level of responsibility is not new. Self-directed teams were introduced in the United States in the 1960s by companies like Procter & Gamble. Holacracy takes this idea several steps further by eliminating most of the supervisory and management positions and replacing them with group decision-making processes.

The constellation practice group members were familiar with the company either as customers or through the media. None of them, however, had any insider information about the change process beyond what was reported. They did know that until the results were either validated or discounted by a company insider or an article in a business journal, the case study had to be treated as conjecture.

Our source material was limited to recent articles and a couple of books about the company. The sources agreed that the workplace culture was what defined the company and enabled it to deliver great customer service. They quoted employees who believed passionately in *"working well together to create an environment that is welcoming and inspiring."* Stodgy, uptight corporate America this place was not. Yet, the initiative to implement Holacracy was not welcomed by everyone with cheers. According to some media reports, 14 percent of the staff took a three-month severance package offered to those who felt self-management was not for them. Clearly, the company CEO was ready to risk the engagement and productivity the old culture delivered for the rewards the new structure promised. Were those who stayed ready to sip the Kool-Aid?

To start the constellation process, six parts of the change process were defined as essential: the CEO, employees who were committed to the change, employees who were not committed, Holacracy, hidden agendas, and the new culture/benefits Holacracy was supposed to produce. The participants in the practice group selected their part of the system and found their place in relationship to one another. At first the hidden agendas faced Holacracy and stood between it and both the new culture and the employees. Hidden agendas expressed with a smirk that Holacracy was just the latest pretty face people were taken with. When the committed employees and new culture retorted they were strong enough to deal with obstacles related to Holacracy, the hidden agendas felt compelled to step to the side. The uncommitted employees joined hidden agendas, and, along with new culture and committed employees, they looked toward the CEO for his guidance.

The CEO in the constellation, however, seemed oddly detached. When asked by the committed employees what they should do, he replied he wanted them to figure that out. Every question they asked received the stock reply that he was observing the process and did not want to interfere. This had a disquieting effect. The committed employees and new culture insisted they needed his leadership. The uncommitted employees were more critical and complained he was uninvolved and disconnected. "You can't make this a social experiment and wait to see what happens. We need to feel you are with us," they told him. The CEO did seem confused and uncertain. How could people expect to be empowered if he didn't give them the space to make their own decisions? He admitted he felt weak.

Holacracy moved back a few feet from the CEO. She felt this was an issue the CEO and his employees needed to work out on their own. Discussing any significant topic would be fruitless until they redefined their expectations of each other. The committed employees were disheartened and turned away. New culture looked chagrined. The CEO moved closer to the employees, but their level of distress did not diminish. A representative was placed next to the CEO on the floor as the source of this alienation between him and the others. The representative looked at the CEO with questioning eyes. "Am I to live or die?" he asked. The CEO looked back and forth at the new culture, who stood nearby, and the old culture, who was on the floor beside him. "You can't have both," the old culture said. "The old has to pass away if the new is going to take its place."

"I don't want to let you go," the CEO sighed. "I didn't realize how attached I was. It's hard, but I let you go." The old culture withdrew. The CEO took the hands of both groups of employees as well as of the new culture. Holacracy came over to join them. "You needed me and I wasn't there for you," he said tearfully. "We are all in this together and I am here for you now." All the representatives began to smile. "When you connect with us in this way, vulnerable and real, we can be a part of this and believe it will work," they told him. The constellation ended on a note of confidence; no one was holding back and they were all in this together.

**Reflections:** The statement "The king is dead, long live the king" mirrors the conundrum facing a company as it moves to embrace self-management. The king for this company, its organizing principle, has been its unique culture and the exceptional customer service it fosters. Inevitably, for the new culture to arrive the old has to depart. Naturally, there will be tremendous concern about breaking something that is not only not broke but also the source of what made the company great. Before people can really let go, they often have to acknowledge their sadness over "what was." Giving space, perhaps even ceremonial space and ritual, for the feelings of confusion, grief, and anger is necessary before there is acceptance and the readiness to move on.

Managing change is about wrestling with paradox.

Holacracy is a new concept. Consultants can help, but each company has to unravel the mystery and risk of implementation. During times of change and uncertainty, people look for strong leadership. Holacracy, however, is based on the expectation that people can do a better job leading themselves when the hierarchy gets out of the way. The resolution to this standoff appeared when the CEO in our constellation realized he was still attached to the original culture his company was built upon. Letting go of what was dearly beloved was the price for moving forward.

Another part of the paradox in establishing a manager-less company is that in times of uncertainty people want answers. Just how long it will take to establish the new normal is one of the many unknowns. Employees look to management to provide strong leadership. The new expectation, however, is that everyone should figure things out together when clarity is elusive. If this expectation is understood and supported with the necessary level of leadership the road to the new normal would still be bumpy but perhaps less painful.

**More Reflections:** If it's not broke why break it? During a review of this case study, this question was pondered. One perceptive colleague noted that under the CEO's leadership it was likely his employees gained a deep felt-sense of belonging as family. This level of kinship in the workplace has never been ingrained in the United States as it is in many other cultures, so they found something they did not know was missing. The CEO, regarded by some as a charismatic genius, was ready to risk the exceptional to achieve the extraordinary. Holacracy just might be the next level of organizational evolution made possible by mobile connectivity and smartphone apps. In terms of Spiral Dynamics, the CEO was seeking to take his "Green" organization, based on affiliation and sharing, and transform it into one that was a transpersonal and holistic "Teal."[1]

Spiral Dynamics is a complex model of human and social evolution with a lot of colors representing different levels of development. No matter what color is used to represent the stage of development where Holacracy is viable, eliminating the managers could prove to be either a farsighted idea or a quixotic setback. The unconscious role of the CEO as the benevolent father who fostered a big, happy family was now something different. For some employees, perhaps, he had become the absent or detached father who left his adolescents alone and unguided while they struggled to become adults. The way to adulthood is to figure things out on your own, yet, paradoxically, sage guidance is sometimes needed. This could be the classic archetype of the visionary, rushing headlong toward the unknowable, new world while those who reluctantly voyage with him yearn for what was forsaken. Both the impatient visionary and the reluctant explorers would be wise to appreciate the angst or urgency the other feels in the tension between what was and what could be.

### Empathy Mapping

One way to get a snapshot of a group is through empathy mapping. A facilitator interviews the team members and reconstructs their worldview based on how events shaped their shared reality. Outsiders might see someone who has a negative attitude and a lack of engagement. If the outsiders could understand where the attitude and actions came from they might be better able to relate to that person. Thoughts and emotions that result from a trauma can shape a person's worldview. Behaviors habitually based on that worldview can become self-fulfilling and repetitive. If someone sees himself as a blameless victim, the reality of that frozen past can determine his future. Judging others will not break this ingrained point of view. Understanding based on empathy might. Adapting the stance of personal responsibility and cocreation starts with small steps that are possible when the person or group feel they have been seen and heard.

An internal team coach was working with a group that had been locked into a downward cycle for years. People stayed even though they were miserable. Although the group's performance was substandard, the culture of the larger organization kept it from being disbanded. A long succession of managers had come and gone yet morale and performance remained low. The newest manager had been on the job just a few months when he suffered a health issue and took a medical leave of absence. During his absence his boss, the director, supervised the group, gaining a small degree of trust. The manager eventually returned to duty, still overwhelmed by the depth of what he was up against.

The director asked the coach to help the new manager address the long-standing issues. The coach was skeptical. Previous off-site retreats and trainings had had no discernable impact. Looking for a new way forward he selected, at a public workshop, representatives for the manager, the director, the team, and himself and set them up as shown in Figure 10-18.

The representative for the manager stood frozen in pain and distress. The *director* appeared attentive but seemed unable to help. The *team* looked out the window; first they were distracted and unconcerned and then they projected a mood of boredom and alienation. A generalized sense of pain in the room grew increasingly tangible. I asked the representatives to stay with that tension

**Figure 10-18**

and move as they felt inspired. The *coach* seemed unable to connect with the director, the manager, or the team in a meaningful way. He walked restlessly back and forth. The *director* moved closer to the *manager*. The *manager* stayed frozen, hardly noticing anything around him. The *team* wandered off to look at a door—perhaps, metaphorically, seeking a way out.

I had the *coach* tell the *director* and the *manager*, "This situation is your responsibility. I can help you but you have to fix it." The mood lightened slightly as if the two leaders accepted something they had tried to avoid. The *director* and coach then said to the *manager*, "We are with you. You don't have to do this alone." The *manager* sighed and relaxed, admitting that he had felt the weight of the world on his shoulders. The *director* replied, "You don't have to carry it all by yourself. You can ask for help." The *manager* felt better and was now able to see the others.

The director and the manager and the *coach* started to approach the *team*, which had now turned to face them. I told them to wait. They needed a plan that would bring all the people together. A compelling purpose was introduced and its representative stood beside them beaming. The four of them moved closer to the *team,* which surveyed them warily. The *director* spoke about the new purpose that would unite them. The *team* was unimpressed and unresponsive. One of the observers moved closer so she could hear the conversation. I asked her to be the voice of the team. She reported she had heard all those promises before; it was just blah, blah, blah.

The director, the manager, and the *purpose* looked stymied. While they wondered how to respond, another observer came and stood by the team. He had been feeling unexpectedly sleepy during the constellation. As a facilitator he knew this was a sign of unexpressed pain. While he stood next to the team, I asked the director and the manager to acknowledge what they saw. They needed to appreciate the difficulties the team had endured. For the first time the team's representative softened and nodded. This was the starting place for rebuilding the relationships: not trying to fix things, just being present with the team and their pain.

**Reflections:** I suggested that the coach conduct a timeline exercise with the team. On a wall or series of flip charts they would list the significant events that occurred during the life of the team. The director and manager needed to look at what had occurred, and its emotional impact, but not be overwhelmed by it. After this mapping exercise the team would likely have more capacity to reengage in their work and achieve the expected standards.

## Chapter 11
# Family Business Challenges

n some ways, every business is a family business. This happens unconsciously when the unresolved dynamics of our family of origin are projected onto our boss and coworkers. In a family business all the traumas and dramas of the past and the present reinforce each other since the principal employees belong to the same family tree. One of the perennial issues is succession. Turning over control to the next generation is predictably a bumpy process whether or not the rising managers are ready to take charge.

### Family Feud

Mae, the office manager in a small, family-owned business, was frustrated by the behavior of the family members and the impact that had on her productivity. The owners/CEOs, a married couple, were semiretired—or claimed they were. Like many company founders, however, they could not let go of the day-to-day details. When they returned from a trip, it took a lot of the office manager's time to help them catch up on those details. Their son, the vice president, was supposed to be taking over as the CEO, yet he had a lackadaisical attitude. He deferred to his parents when they were around but did not take charge when they were not. The head of production was the son-in-law of the owners/CEOs. He was more focused than the VP was, but he was not empowered by his brother-in-law or father-in-law to make decisions. The supervisor, like Mae, was not a member of the family. He and she tried their best to skirt the vortex of family politics and remain on good terms with the other four.

Mae felt irritated with the company's founders for their "seagull" style of management: dropping things on her, flying away, and then returning to drop more. She got along reasonably well with the supervisor, but most of his time was spent in the field. She was frustrated by the lack of leadership on the part of the VP. I asked Mae if she would lose her job if she spoke up. Would the business go bankrupt if she did not? Would things muddle along even if people continued to act the same way? Maybe, maybe, and maybe. None of her options seemed attractive. She appreciated the son-in-law's work ethic yet wished he were more proactive and savvy in working out the differences between himself and his brother-in-law. I asked her to reflect on the part she, as the office manager, played in maintaining this dysfunctional system. If she changed, how might the others have to change as well? Mae selected representatives and set them up as shown in Figure 11-1.

The place for Mae to start was at the top. I asked her to honor the owners/CEOs as the founders of the business. She thanked them for starting the business and giving her a job. She appreciated their vision and the years of hard work they put into the business to achieve it. Their

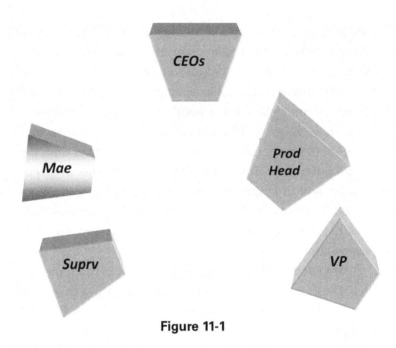

**Figure 11-1**

contribution as the founders would be remembered with a photograph displayed in the office. She told the *vice president* she appreciated his role in ensuring the success of the company. He was the boss and she was his employee; she looked to him to make the right decisions. To the *son-in-law,* she said how much she appreciated his work ethic and desire to succeed. He could count on her to help his good work to be recognized and appreciated. She expressed the same sentiments to the *supervisor.*

Thereafter, the group was rearranged so that everyone had their place within the company leadership, starting with the most senior persons on the left, as seen in Figure 11-2.

I placed a representative for a company vision where they could each see it. Each one of them separately and collectively played a role in achieving that vision and keeping the business healthy and prosperous.

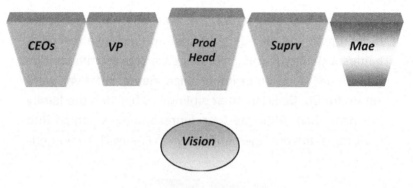

Figure 11-2

**Reflections:** Mae left with a better understanding about what was behind the dynamics with the family business. If the family members were clear about and aligned around the firm's vision, the owners/CEOs could find it easier to turn their title and duties over to the VP. While there were things Mae could do on her own, like honoring the founders, it would still be up to the family members to change their ways. If she agreed to "what is" she would have more energy available to choose a different path for herself. Unlike with her own family of origin, she could decide to stay or to leave. The feeling that she was not free to leave would indicate an overlap between the dynamics showing up in the business and those that were in her own family of origin. Surfacing any unconscious connection between the two would be her key to freedom and personal choice.

### Gripping the Purse

As we saw in the previous case study, parents in a family business tend to hold on to the decision-making responsibilities long past the time they are to be passed to their children. This can happen even when the next generation is prepared and ready to take over. Ceil, a woman in her late thirties who worked in her father's company, was dealing with this issue. Her father, Ed, was open-minded about most things and talked about sharing executive responsibilities with his children. In practice, he kept a white-knuckle grip on any decision of importance. Representatives were set up for Ed, Ceil, the other siblings (Sibs), and the family business (Biz). After the four representatives settled into their roles, the arrangement shown in Figure 11-3 emerged.

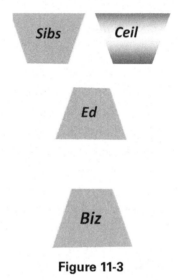

**Figure 11-3**

*Ed's* representative reported that he felt protective of the business (Biz). The kids were still kids in his eyes. The *siblings* and, to some extent, *Ceil* felt frustrated. They had paid their dues and had proved they were ready to take over. This meant nothing if their father refused to follow through. The business felt okay about the situation and interested in how things would turn out.

I had the *siblings* and *Ceil* tell *Ed* they respected and admired him as the steward of the business. They reassured him that his contribution would not be forgotten and he would always have a place of honor in their hearts. *Ed's* stance softened in response, yet he remained protective of his business, which had been founded by Ceil's great-grandmother at the beginning of the twentieth century. She passed it on to her son, Ed's father. Representatives for Ceil's great-grandmother and grandfather were placed in the constellation. *Ed* was asked to face his father. *Ed* appeared smaller, as if he was now in the role of being the child who did not have the confidence of his parent. *Ceil's grandfather* turned and faced his mother (Ceil's great-grandmother). He honored her role in founding the business and thanked *her* for passing it on to him. *She* handed him a purse, one that actually did belong to Ceil, to symbolize the responsibility for running the business.

*Ed's* father passed *Ed* the purse. *Ed* held out the purse to his children but did not let go of it. *He* felt better about letting them participate in running the company but wondered if they could handle all the responsibility by themselves. Ed's children took hold of the purse that *Ed* still gripped. *Ceil* and *her siblings* promised to keep an honored place for him in the company. His voice would be heard when any important matter needed to be considered. They asked for his blessing and the opportunity to become the stewards and leaders he had modeled for them. Ed slowly and wordlessly let go of the purse.

**Reflections:** The turnover of control from one generation will be smoother if the younger generation actively recognizes and honors the accomplishments of their elders. The role of the parents is to prepare their children to become autonomous adults. If they withhold the reins of responsibility for too long they keep their adult children in a state of childlike dependence. Ceil's task was to find a way for her and her siblings to both publicly and privately acknowledge the stewardship of their father and his lineage. Her father may have been reenacting how his own transition to a place of leadership unfolded with his father years earlier. It is part of the natural order for the parents to give and the children to receive.[1] One sign that something has disrupted this flow of giving and receiving is a lack of honoring. Expressions of gratitude, appreciation, respect, and blessing are all means for restoring this natural flow.

Joseph Campbell once said, *"If you want to change the world, you have to change the metaphor."*[2] We know that Madison Avenue is constantly barraging us with symbolic images that influence our beliefs and behaviors in ways we hardly realize.[3] Imagery and symbols are powerful ways to speak to the subconscious. The metaphor of handing over the purse from parent to child is emotionally evocative. If Ceil could inspire her family to conduct a ritual with the relevant symbolism and expressions that affirmed and celebrated the transition from one generation to the next it might help her father let go.

## Chapter 12

# Management Constellations

The term "management constellation" is used when facilitating a business team whose members work with each other.[1] Most of the constellations described so far in this book took place with participants who were strangers before they met at the workshop. Anonymity makes it easier to discuss the issues people have with others who are not in the room. Although the cloak of anonymity and distance is lost with an intact team, the constellation process can still be incredibly helpful. Often, I don't bother to name the process or explain the theory behind what I am asking an intact group to do. They don't care anyway. They are just interested in solutions and insights related to their problems. When I make the mistake of trying to explain too much, pretty quickly people's eyes roll back indicating it is time to shift from words to actions.

## Be Cautiously Bold

As with any facilitated exercise, just how much you can challenge the intact group depends on your relationship with them. The more trust and familiarity you have, the more likely they will give what you suggest a try even if it seems unusual, silly, or—heaven forbid—touchy-feely. When you are confident and comfortable with the process and yourself, it's likely they will be too. A critical difference between an intact and a non-intact group is that the stakes are higher for the former. Inherently, you will be helping them deal with one or more of their group issues. Since their interactions continue after you leave it's crucial to make sure you select the right tools for their discussions. A constellation may not be that tool, especially if anonymity and confidentially are required. If the intact group is assessing a system, those parts are mostly outside the room, as in the case study later in the chapter titled "Kids Rule." A conversation about harmonizing those parts has a higher level of emotional safety than does one in which all the actual, real-life parts are in the room, as in the following case study, "Real-Life Organogram."

A traditional constellation can be like an X-ray that exposes what people are actually thinking and feeling. It bears repeating that you need to know your intact group, especially their hot buttons and the group's readiness to discuss them, before you begin constellating. Not doing your homework and adjusting the session design accordingly could have unforeseen and even undesirable consequences. The more you assess and adjust before you leap the better. The case studies in this chapter demonstrate various ways you can marry systems thinking with the knowing field. The resulting offspring of insights and solutions will raise the group's energy and enthusiasm. In management constellations, the group, rather than an individual, is normally the issue holder. Consequently, the issue holders in this chapter are not highlighted as is the case with the other types of constellations in this book.

## The Real-Life Organogram

I have used this systemic exercise at numerous corporate retreats for over a decade. The Real-Life Organogram is a consistent winner because no matter how long people have been working together, they come away with a more solid sense of themselves and how they are organized. When people look at the organization chart they create and viscerally feel their place and the place of their coworkers, it helps them coalesce as a group. Moving from the theoretical to the actual affirms something in both the individual and the collective mind. It also offers those who seldom have a chance to be seen or heard by others the opportunity for both. If the group is large—that is, more than forty people—I usually project their org chart as a PowerPoint slide and ask the group to stand in their working groups as if they were creating a physical chart that matches the one on the screen. The typical group forms up as shown in Figure 12-1, which includes an administrative section that reports to the front office.

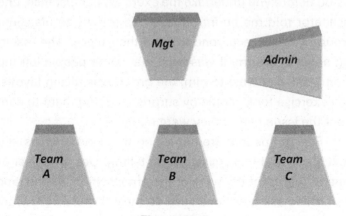

**Figure 12-1**

Once people find their place in the organogram the team leaders and manager each say a few words about their role, the work of their team, and how they interact with others. Depending on the time available and the size of the group, all the participants might be asked to briefly describe their individual roles. This is valuable in that often people are mystified by what others are doing all day. They relish the opportunity to be seen and to see their fellow workers. Don't be surprised if a few people don't know where they belong. Briefly explore their options and find them a home even if it is temporary.

Sometimes it just so happens that everyone is confused. People mill about unsure where to stand or who to stand with. Groups organized as a matrix are prone to this type of confusion, and as a result, they will benefit especially from a discussion about reporting lines and workflow. When a problem like this is embodied graphically, everyone sees it and feels it in the moment. A solution is more likely to emerge because the graphically demonstrated issue is easier for a group to grasp. While the success rate of this activity has been 100 percent, it is always wise to know your group and the issues the members are facing before you undertake the exercise. For instance, one facilitator told me he introduced this activity to his client group by telling everyone to "find their place." The resulting angst and turmoil was such that some people left the room. Unbeknownst to him, the group was facing layoffs. The exercise took people by surprise, forcing them to confront the issue before they were ready to.

For groups that are not facing that kind of crisis, the next stage of the exercise can be telling. Use an object or tape to represent the work of the organization. As the tape is unrolled ask questions such as these: Where does work come in? Who is it passed to? How is quality maintained?

A unit can be organized one way on paper, but that does not mean the territory is like the map. No matter what you were told, what shows up in real time is the reality the group needs to examine. At a retreat for a large international organization, I used a large roll of red engineer's tape to map the workflow of a typical project. By the end of the exercise, the designated project manager was wrapped up like a mummy in the tape that crisscrossed the entire group. Still draped in that red tape, the project manager opened the discussion by declaring that this was the best day of his life. There was no refuting the fractured process everyone had just seen. The exercise inspired the formation of a working group to streamline project coordination between different departments.

## Real-Time Strategic Change

A well-known methodology known as Real-Time Strategic Change brings together the leaders from all parts of an extended corporate system to discuss what is working and what needs to be changed.[2] This is not cheap. Flying in partners, stakeholders, vendors, and clients who are external to the organization, as well as the core players within it—all of whom are spread about geographically—can be financially daunting. One way around the constraints of time and money is to map the entire system with a smaller number of people who are easy to convene. In the following four case studies, I simply asked the core group I was facilitating to represent the different subgroups in their extended system. Each subgroup sat at its own table and discussed the issue from their point of view.

People would typically surprise themselves with what they didn't know they knew. New information emerged from the mapping that all the participants could see and comment on. The visually inspired insights helped the groups realize authentic agreements and committed actions.

## ISO World-Class Status

One off-site session I conducted was with the leadership team of the logistical support department that had local offices in a number of second and third world countries. Given the global nature of her enterprise, the leader's overarching goal was to be "world-class" in their efficiency, effectiveness, and customer service. During the session, I suggested that we do an "organizational mapping" exercise to look at the major elements of their system and how the relationships between them could be optimized. Eight parts to the system were identified, starting with the vice president for their division and the manager for their department. The parts were arranged to represent the current status. The initial configuration (pictured in Figure 12-2) was adjusted step-by-step as the discussion progressed.

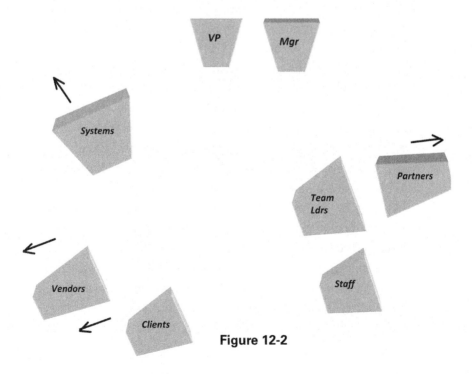

**Figure 12-2**

The arrows next to some of the representatives indicate that their distance from the center of the constellation was greater than can be shown to scale.

Once the representatives found their places the first thing that stood out was their distance from each other. (The *vendors, clients,* and *partners*, especially, were farther away from the core staff than there is room to show in the diagram.) The *vendors* reported feeling disconnected and uncertain about their place. Who did they turn to when they needed information or assistance? The *clients* also felt on their own and uncertain about the service they would receive. Was the logistical system there to help or to hinder them? Would they get into trouble if they got too close to their vendors? *Partners* stood some distance behind *staff* and facing away from them. Only when contacted by others would their representative turn around and engage.

Systems (IT, records and knowledge management, office and project procedures) were also further back. *Systems* was confused about whom she belonged to. Everyone needed to connect to her, but each group's needs were different. Where did she face? Who was her master? How could she provide good data if the data were not entered properly?

All could see that the status quo that was presenting itself was far from world-class. During the dialogue that followed, responsibilities were clarified, requests and offerings were made, and specific actions were outlined that would restore or foster order in the organizational system between the different groups.

As the representatives discussed those actions, their actual physical movements responded to their dialogue. They moved closer and faced each other more directly. As Jakob Schneider, a well-known constellation facilitator, states, *"A relationship system is in order when all the representatives have found a place that feels right."*[3] Adding a representative for the purpose of the department helped strengthen the group's alignment around the goal of being world-class. Highlighting their collective purpose increased the sense of engagement the parts had with each other and reduced the sense of distance and isolation that at first characterized their relationships.

**Reflections:** The list of actions that came out of the exercise provided the manager with an outline for advancing toward her stated goal. The purpose of the department and its rationale for seeking to be world-class was an element that had been overlooked. Their clients were involved in reforming governmental operations and reducing corruption and inefficiency in middle- and low-income countries. Because of their potential for making a difference in people's lives, the department had an obligation to lead by example. This required more communication, participation, and alignment between the parts of their organization than they currently possessed. Interestingly, even though the leadership of the unit later changed, being a global example remained a consistent theme. The new manager recounted his own personal experiences that fostered his conviction about why the department could and should set the example on the global stage.

## The Structure of Stewardship

Sidney was the leader of a professional services firm that he had founded more than thirty years ago. His goal was to retire in a year or two and cash out the equity in his firm. No one, including Sidney, wanted him to sell the firm to an outsider or another organization. The employees appreciated their unique culture, which they characterized as caring, nurturing, and supportive. They believed that the high level of positivity in the firm also fostered a high level of productivity. Turnover was low and profitability, which included profit sharing, exceeded the industry norm. People worried that Sidney was irreplaceable: if he left, the culture of nurturing and mutual support they all enjoyed might leave with him.

Sidney's vision was for the firm to continue to be successful through the shared leadership of all the staff, both professional and administrative. The question was, what kind of structure and process would enable that level of shared leadership and responsibility? Sidney's executive foresight and knack for being two steps ahead of a typical workplace dilemma was not something you learn in an MBA program. If someone from the outside did buy Sidney's shares, the organization was sure to change to reflect the personality of the new owner. If staff found a way to take ownership as a group, change would still occur, but they would have more of a say in what those changes would be. They reviewed their options for restructuring the firm and came up with four:

❐ **Corporate:** the percentage earned is based on seniority and valued added
❐ **Collaborative:** a market umbrella that would charge sublease fees
❐ **Cooperative:** shared ownership that all members buy into
❐ **Holacracy:** a self-governing entity with roles and decision-making processes defined by a charter.[4] (For a case study about Holacracy in action, look at "Organizational Evolution" in chapter 10, which deals entirely with organizational constellations.)

There was no consensus about the most desirable structure. The current structure was a mix of corporate and collaborative. The professionals were paid a percentage of the billings they produced. Administrative staff was paid a set salary out of overhead. Sidney took some small percentage of profits, but mostly saw his return in terms of the equity he was building up. After a detailed discussion about the pros and cons of each option, I suggested we explore the issue through a process that was more somatic than mental. I told them we would let our minds take a coffee break since they had been concentrating hard all morning. In the exercise we would rely on our bodies and emotions; that felt-sense that our intuition uses to let us know when something seems right or not.

I took a piece of paper that had the firm's name written on it, along with their vision for a successful future, and laid it on the floor in the center of the large room we were in. Representatives were selected at random and handed a notecard inscribed with an aspect of the firm or one of the structural options. They were told not to look at their note-cards until asked and trust that their subconscious would know where they should go in the room. For most it was their first constellation, yet they took to it without a glance of surprise. After two or three minutes of wandering about, they ended up as shown in Figure 12-3.

Once they found their spot in the room I asked each representative in turn to report out what they noticed or felt. The structure of *collaboration* clearly had the strongest connection and interest in the new *vision. Clients* and the desired *culture* also reported that their energy and interest were directed toward the *vision.* Both *corporate* and *cooperative* structures were taken up with looking out the large windows in the room. They gazed at how the light was reflecting off the trees. *Holacracy* took notice of them

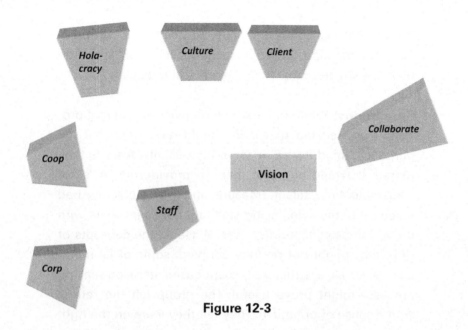

**Figure 12-3**

but also kept an eye on what the other side of the room was doing. *Staff* took a seat on the floor and looked toward vision with a meditative gaze.

The representatives discussed what they felt toward each other and the new vision from the perspective of where they had placed themselves in the room. Since this was a blind constellation they did not know what part they were assigned and only stated what they noticed in the moment. I explained that we used this format when we wanted to be sure to keep the mind out of the knowing process and rely on our subconscious. After they looked at their papers, we discussed the image that had emerged. The previous structure, a combination of corporate and cooperative, did not appear to have a connection to the future of the firm. *Staff* had been seated on the floor facing the vision. This raised the question whether they would stand up to the challenge of making the vision and new structure a reality. The option closest to the *vision* was *collaborative.* There was a direct

line of sight that connected *staff,* the *vision,* and *collabora-*
*tion.* Collaboration, according to the constellation, appeared
to be the structure that held the greatest potential.

**Reflections:** While the restructuring was an internal process, I pointed out that staff should remember that the
purpose behind it was to serve their clients. After Sidney
retired, it would be up to them to provide the "4T's" of
leadership: time, talent, treasure, and trust. Holacracy had
stood off to the side, facing staff and not as involved with
the vision as collaboration was. While all the concepts of
Holacracy might not be fully adopted, some of its methods—such as a structured, team-based decision-making
process—might prove useful. The group left the retreat
with a sense of optimism. They felt they were on the right
path toward the collegial restructuring of their firm. Their
shared sense of efficacy in dealing with Sidney's retirement was strengthened. Most important, they felt more
confident about their ability as a group to make the coming
decision and implement it.

### Kids Rule

A government ministry for education in a less developed country was put in charge of organizing a new national
"head start" program for kindergartners.

A retreat was scheduled to strengthen policy-setting
functions, conduct strategic and implementation planning,
and achieve the level of teamwork needed to implement
the new program. The amount of information my co-facil-
itator and I had was sketchy, so we met in-country before
the retreat and traveled to the conference center where it
would be held to conduct a planning constellation. Sitting
on a narrow beach littered by trash we made a smooth
place in the sand to map the different part of the ministry

and its current dynamics. We had heard there was a conflict between two key individuals who would be attending. How might this affect the proceedings? How could it be mitigated?

Using small sticks stuck in the sand we placed the different participants and groups in relationship to each other. Reporting out was done by touching a stick and giving voice to what the person or group it represented might have to say. Using this process it appeared that the minister's attention was focused on areas other than starting up this new program. The different groups faced away from each other, seemingly to pursue their own agendas. Were different visions behind some of the tensions? Did different communication styles add to those differences? Three actions seemed to be called for. First, establishing the norms of mutual respect through reflective listening. Second, creating together a clear and authentic vision to unify the efforts of the different groups. Third, facilitating an interactive session on understanding different communication styles.

The next day forty participants arrived at the conference center. A viable strategic plan was expected to emerge from their discussions. How could the concerns and suggestions of stakeholders and partners in the new program become part of this process? All the participants were mid- or senior-level staff from the ministry. There were no recent polls or surveys to draw upon. The lack of stakeholder data was not ideal, but just getting the ministry staff to the conference was a victory of sorts. To fill in the gaps we decided to draw upon the tacit knowledge of the participants. At the beginning of the planning process, five small groups were formed at random. Each group represented the voice of a stakeholder in the educational system that needed to be heard. The five small groups diagrammed in Figure 12-4

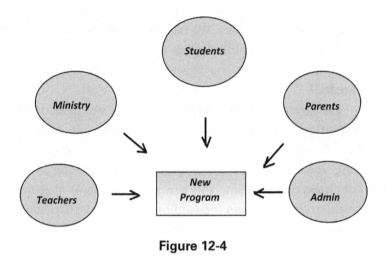

**Figure 12-4**

each had their perspective on what success for the new program would look like.

The stakeholder groups prepared presentations on their wants, needs, and concerns related to the new program. All the members in each group were asked to participate to enliven the skit-like format. As the groups took turns in the front of the room, the feeling grew stronger that the information provided truly gave voice to what the actual stakeholders would have communicated. The groups included the ministry, teachers, parents, school administrators, and, of course, the kindergartners. The presentations were lighthearted and playful, especially when the kindergartners took their turn. Comparing and contrasting the different perspectives helped identify interconnected issues that needed to be addressed. Each group wrote their goals on a flip chart. When lined up side by side, the combined goals unexpectedly turned out to be the shared vision of the program they had been looking for.

**Reflections:** This exercise was a high point for all the participants. Space had been made for their differences and the related emotions to be expressed. They were delighted they had managed a dialogue not only without blame but also with humor and goodwill. Although the minister spent much of his time on his cell phone, he did listen to and affirm his commitment to the vision the unit had created. At the end of the retreat, as participants shared what they were taking away, a surprising comment was made. One of the two leaders who had had the strained relationship stood up and said that he did not know exactly why or how it had happened, but now he felt that he and his colleague could work together and he was looking forward to a new relationship.

During the retreat we did not spend time explaining the dynamics or theory behind the exercises. The participants discovered for themselves the benefit in representing and giving voice to the different parts of the national kindergarten program. Somewhat tongue in cheek we classified our exercise with the table groups as a covert constellation. What was important, though, was that the results were overt since they were making visible the information they did not know they knew.

## New Messages for a New Plan

A department in an international organization was going through a period of significant change. There was a new manager, considerable turnover in staff, and a pressing need to redefine both the general strategy and the operational plans for specific countries. A management constellation was conducted at the department's planning retreat to gain insight into how best to manage the recent changes. Representatives for the elements within and external to the department were identified and set up. These numerous elements included: national governments in third world countries; citizen clients in those countries who benefited from the services their government provided; HQ, staff and country management (Cty Mgt) and staff (Cty Staff) in the country offices; the desired development results; the department manager; the new strategic plan; other partners in development; and financial donors. The organizing question was, "How can this complex system be optimally organized to produce the desired results?" I explained to the participants that we first had to set up and acknowledge the "real" before there could be movement toward the "ideal."

Representatives for the system were selected and positioned physically to illustrate the functionality of their relationships. Their positions, shown in Figure 12-5, illustrated two disconnects.

First, the staff and management had different visions of what they hoped to accomplish and how to do it. The representatives reported this somatically and their relative positions in the constellation demonstrated it physically. This was no surprise because of the many recent changes they had been through. Making the new business plan a collaborative process would hopefully foster alignment between the various groups. The second revelation was a bigger concern. As the representatives interacted and reported out, it became obvious that the department was not connected in a meaningful way to its partners and clients and the results they were seeking.

Government clients had a long history of other priorities that, rightly or not, made it difficult to get their attention. The current period of transition meant some degree of looking inward was needed. For the department to be effective, however, more direct engagement with its clients was crucial. The more coherent and unified the department became internally, the more successful it could be externally in strengthening client and partner relationships. As

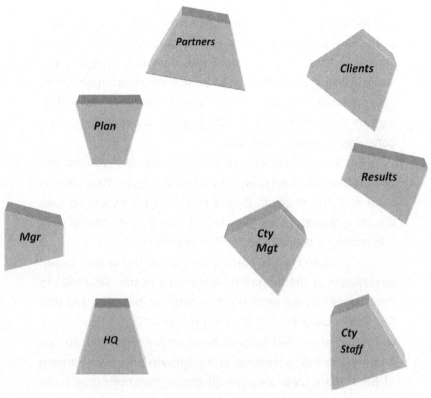

**Figure 12-5**

the representatives continued to interact in the constellation, the complexity of the system became overwhelming. The manager, as he observed the confusion, dryly commented, "This looks like a mess, so what we have to remember are the principles that guide our work."

Shared principles was the glue that would bond together the fragmented parts of the department. One obstacle in the way of unity was scarcity thinking. The principle "There is enough work and recognition for everyone, especially if we work together" needed to be modeled by senior staff. It was crucial that all staff felt that they had a respected and valued place within the department. A calming message for specialists from the senior staff was "We will look to you first, before others outside the unit, when projects are staffed." This was a sensitive topic. Some senior staff felt that the time they spent developing and supervising specialists placed an extra burden upon them. The specialists believed they would not grow as professionals if the senior staff opted to use more experienced consultants instead of them.

For administrative staff, the principle was "You are and will be treated as an integral part of our team. Your work is seen and appreciated." It was common for others to take the administrators for granted or leave them in the dark concerning a project they were supporting.

In a related issue, communication with the staff based overseas was challenged by distance and the difference in time zones. Better working relationships between HQ and the field would flow from the principle "Don't hesitate to call when you need help or have an idea. We will do our best to respond." Investing in the growth and development of field office staff also would strengthen their credibility with the host government and enable them to better support the HQ staff when they were in-country.

Representatives for the international donors who funded the department's projects were added to the systemic map. Their message to staff was to appreciate who they were serving and to keep in mind their role of facilitating the interactions between everyone engaged in a development project. The spirit of humility and respect was essential. A story was shared about a European government that sent an "expert" to a country in the Middle East. The expert turned out to have nothing to contribute to the development project. The fallout from that assignment demonstrated the consequences of not appreciating the level of expertise already possessed by the host government. To gain the attention and goodwill of their clients, the principle the department needed to embrace was "We are honored to be of service to you and those who use your public services. We value your knowledge and experience."

**Reflections:** The issues being addressed by this department were perennial works in progress throughout the larger institution. It was a well-known precept that the quality of relationships determined the quality of the results. I suggested to the manager it would be wise to keep revisiting and reinforcing these underlying principles. The more staff internalized them in spirit and deed, the more likely they would strengthen their relationships throughout the entire system.

## You're One of Us

At the beginning of a leadership course I led for a large organization, the participants explored a work-related goal. They formed pairs. One person was the goal and the other person the subject, who found his place in relationship to the goal. The subjects were asked to notice how they felt about their goal and to find out how it felt about them. One pair was a middle-aged white man and a young black woman who was physically much smaller than the man. During the debriefing of the exercise, he mentioned he felt the need not to loom over her. He was concerned that not only his size but also his race and gender might seem intimidating. This touched his partner. Tearfully, she shared that even though she had graduated from a well-known university and spoke several languages, people in the workplace did not always take her seriously. She was that "black girl," and she believed ageism, sexism, and racism kept some of her colleagues from seeing and appreciating her capabilities.

The collective presence in the room deepened in

response to her heartfelt sharing. I asked the group to stay present with the emotions they and the young woman were feeling without trying to fix anything. Then I asked the young woman if she was willing to look around the circle and take in the kindness in the expressions of her class-mates. She tried to look up and take it in but indicated it wasn't safe. Spontaneously, people offered words of empa-thy. A wounding is always worse if we feel we have to bear it alone. Emotional wounds happen in relationship with oth-ers. The healing also happens in relationship with others. The fear of more wounding causes us to isolate ourselves. Yet, the healing could be right there were we able to relate to others and take it in. Seeing others. Letting others see our authentic, unguarded self fosters trust. The South African word "Ubuntu" captures this moment: *"I am because we are."* We create each other through our relatedness.

The young woman eventually looked around the circle, and twenty people looked back with warmth and understanding. I asked everyone to stand up and look at her and together say, "You are one of us. You belong. You have a place here in our group." She beamed as she took in their words of inclusion. I thanked her for showing all of us what true leadership was about. It was the courage to be vulnerable in front of others. Expressing what needs to said in that vulnerability unites people around their shared humanity. The workplace feels a lot safer when every-one knows they have a place. Communicating to others, especially those who have felt excluded in the past, that "you are one of us" is an act of community building. As we moved to take a break one of the participants asked me in wonder, "Do your programs always start with this kind of intensity?"

### Intact Group Cautions

In an open enrollment workshop, the relative anonymity of the setting and the ground rule "what is said in the room stays in the room" enable the participants to reveal sensitive issues they may have only shared with their closest confidants, if at all. This anonymity does not exist for an intact group that you will work with in a management constellation. Consequently, the issues people feel comfortable exploring will lean toward the impersonal and analytical.

As mentioned before, the sensitivities of an intact group, be it a family or a corporate team, are much higher and carry greater risks as well as rewards. Facilitating an intact group calls for an additional set of skills that comes into play before and after the constellation session. When the management constellation is over, the facilitator often continues to work with the group over a period of time using other methods and techniques. Obtaining insights comes through the constellation. Helping the group implement those insights involves methodologies related to executive coaching or organizational development.

No matter how experienced you are as a facilitator or leader, knowing what you don't know can save you from a lot of trouble. Facilitators who learned to constellate in an open enrollment setting should be mindful that an intact group possesses pitfalls that may not be obvious. Don't assume they will respond to the constellation process like the non-intact groups you worked with the day before. If anything, assume they will not. The first few minutes of establishing your credibility and building rapport are critical. They may be open to trying the process but not particularly open to letting what unfolds touch them in a deep way. It is victory enough if the participants in a management constellation create a living image and a felt-sense of the dynamics that exist within their system. This image can jump-start a productive conversation. New ways of looking at a problem will lead to new solutions. As their trust of the process and you, the facilitator, increases, the group will tackle more difficult issues. Don't fret or strain if they don't go as far as you want or expect them to go in the initial session.

Heed the "Go slow to go fast." You know that the felt-sense of a vivid image is enough to engage the subconscious and lead to productive changes. The professionals in the world of business and government, however, tend to be highly educated and impatient for practical results. Like any strength, their ability to analyze can be a liability when overused. Managing the overflow of analysis so it does not interfere with the constellation will be one your challenges. The desire to conceptualize is how people grapple with issues of control and safety. Again, be patient and encourage mindfulness to quiet the overactive mind.

## Chapter 13
# Wicked Problems

Wicked problems are defined as those that are complex, long lasting, and resistant to a variety of solutions. By definition, each wicked problem is unique.

Underlying that uniqueness are the complex dynamics of systems within systems. According to some researchers, people who are limited to linear thinking—about 60 percent of the population—are over their heads when confronted with that level of complexity. Even nonlinear thinkers who can see patterns within a system—about 30 percent of the population—may not be able to grasp the complexity that results when multiple systems interact.[1] The systemic approach offers a multidimensional map that simplifies complex dynamics and brings clarity to an opaque situation. In the following case study, this approach was used as a diagnostic tool to look for causes and solutions related to a well-known and long-running wicked problem in the Washington, DC, area.

### Assessment of the Washington, DC, Metro System

All the constellations in this book took place because someone in a business, either as a manager, staff person, consultant, or principle, had a problem that needed a solution. This constellation was different in that the issue holders were users of the system but not actually part of it as a manager or a team member.

Not every facilitator would agree that this provides the mandate for conducting a constellation. As frequent Metro riders, however, we felt we did have that mandate.

According to the *Washington Post*, since 2002 Washington, DC's, Metro system, the second largest in the country, has accounted for 4 percent of rail track worker fatalities nationwide. As of 2010, there had been seventeen deaths over the previous five years.[2] Passenger and worker injuries and fatalities were higher than in other jurisdictions. The overall level of safety was considered subpar.[3] The question our small group of Metro users asked was, *"Given the safety record what can be done to make the system safer?"*

The problem areas identified in articles and commentary in the local media included aging equipment, procedural noncompliance to safety rules, lack of corrective action in response to past investigations, budget shortfalls, poor communication between management and workers, and fragment oversight between three jurisdictions. The DuPont safety program, begun in 2007, ran for five years to enhance worker skills, abilities, and participation in improving and prioritizing safety. Management oversight, regulations, and public attention had intensified.[4] Various measures to improve safety had been initiated, yet accidents continued to happen. Questions were raised by the public, among them:

❐ Were there sufficient resources, budget, and leadership in place to transform the culture of the Metro and to improve the level of safety?

❐ If so, why was safety still a perennial issue?

Before we started, the participants in the constellation were asked to keep this disclaimer in mind: *"Our findings are hypothetical until they are verified by someone with access to the organization."* We first identified the most tangible parts of the system, such as passengers, workers (staff), management, equipment, the Metro's board, and the Standard Operating Orders (SOOs). The initial layout started with setting up representatives for the parts shown in Figure 13-1.

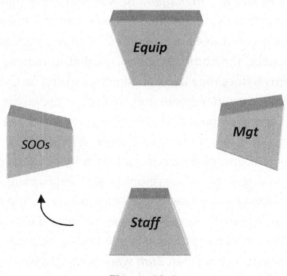

**Figure 13-1**

*Management* reported being pulled in opposing directions. Dealing with equipment was one challenge and the workforce another. Responding to a crisis in one was often interrupted to respond to a problem in the other.

What the Metro called its SOOs were used to coordinate the interface between equipment and staff. *Management* moved next to the *equipment* and faced *staff* directly. *Staff* moved the SOOs away from them, feeling that there should be more space between them and the rules. *Management* reacted with indignation. "What are you doing kicking the rules away? They need to be right next to you."

*Staff* felt that the SOOs were imposed on them without their input or consideration. The more space there was between them and the SOOs, the more comfortable they felt. There was a dichotomy in the system. On one side stood *management* and the rules they imposed on the staff for operating the equipment. On the other stood the *staff,* adamant about protecting their independence and dignity. The more strident *management* was about the rules, the more *staff* felt distrusted and not respected. The rules were a weapon being used against them. Without mutual trust and respect, the communication needed to resolve small problems before they became big ones would be lacking.

What would resolve this apparent stalemate? The distant and disengaged tone of management appeared to belong to the senior level, so a representative for the first and second line of supervisors was added. These supervisors had the role of developing and implementing the SOOs. *Management* was impatiently looking to the supervisors for a plan. The *supervisors* were looking to *management* for a budget. Both sides seemed to be looking for leadership from the other. *Staff* were frustrated with the lack of leadership from both. Instead of being supported, they believed they were being set up for failure. The *supervisors,* however, did feel that staff were, to some extent, unfairly blamed for the safety failures. When *staff* heard this they relaxed and were less oppositional. However, they were still not ready to fully embrace the safety programs being pushed by management. To them, management was more concerned with public relations than with actually protecting anyone's safety. What else needed to be acknowledged or included? Representatives for the accident victims, both workers and passengers, were brought in.

I asked *management* how she felt about the victims. She had little to say to them and even seemed to be resentful, as if they were the source of her troubles.

The *victims* felt that everyone had let them down and betrayed their trust. They were angry, frustrated, and sad. *Staff* asserted that management was trying to put the burden of responsibility for the victims on them. The tension and resentment they felt toward management increased. The representatives thus rearranged themselves as illustrated in Figure 13-2.

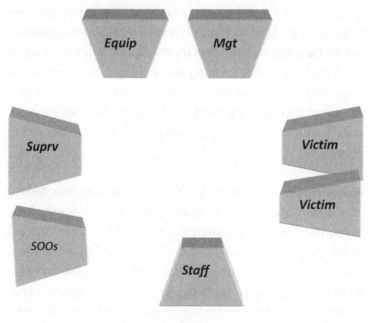

**Figure 13-2**

While the *supervisors* seemed sympathetic toward staff and the victims, nothing would shift as long as *management* tried to distance themselves from the tragedies. *Management* was asked to apologize to the victims and take responsibility for their part in what happened. It took several tries before the managers were able to articulate their role in the tragedies without hedging. After they said they were sorry to the victims and took responsibility, *staff* relaxed and felt friendlier and more respectful toward management. "This is what happens when we don't work together and follow our SOOs," management told *staff* and *supervisors* while pointing toward the *victims.* In response, *staff* felt motivated to move closer to the SOOs and the *supervisors.*

Perhaps even more of a shift would have occurred if the supervisors and staff also had apologized and taken responsibility for their parts. *Management* and *equipment* lined up with *staff* and *supervisors* and faced the passenger and worker *victims.* "We must ensure their safety while we transport them," management told the others while gesturing toward the Metro users. All the parts of the system were then aligned toward this purpose. A felt-sense of unity that had been missing was now present in the entire group.

**Reflections:** According to the constellation, the failure of Metro management to apologize and hold themselves accountable kept the system in a destabilized state. As long as each group felt blamed and disrespected by the others, it would be difficult to come up with and agree to solutions that would address the safety issue. Perhaps, in some unconscious way, each group identified with the victims. While the new safety measures were appropriate, the partnership needed to fully implement them was not viable as long as they hunkered down in their defensive positions.

Staff would be slow to internalize new safety principles if they felt others saw them as needing "fixing." To protect their dignity they resisted the imposition of rules, and they regarded management as the problem. While the issues of aging equipment, noncompliance with SOOs, expansion of the Metro system, political maneuvering, and budget shortfalls all had an impact, by themselves they were not the source of the Metro's woes. Moving from blame to working together might happen if management took responsibility and stopped judging their workers. Once they were accountable then they could ask others to take responsibility for their part.

Articles published in the *Washington Post* after the constellation was conducted were the source for our follow-up. Although the *Post* was emailed a write-up of this constellation, it was doubtful anyone took notice of it. From my reading of the articles, they confirmed the conflict between management and staff and the environment of poor communication.[5] Predictably, new leadership was brought in.[6] Although progress was made in October 2013, there was another death and two injuries in a tunnel explosion thereafter. Surprisingly, a year later the Metro won an award for its improvements in safety.[7] To its credit, a statue it paid for was dedicated to the victims of the Metro accidents.[8] However, safety and service issues continued to arise. The entire system was shut down for a day for emergency safety inspections. Media stories continued to criticize the agency as dysfunctional and a national embarrassment.[9] The Metro's board continues to look for ways to restore the public's faith in the system. That restoration is likely to be more successful when they find a way to end the blame game between management, supervisors, and staff.

# Chapter 14

# Reconciling the Irreconcilable

**G**eopolitical issues, just like our professional or organizational concerns, call for a profound level of understanding if they are going to be resolved. The struggle over resources, geography, and ideology are ingrained in human nature. Social forces behind racial, ethnic, religious, and national conflicts can appear intractable and even inscrutable. The tendency to demonize the other side makes it easier to justify any damage inflicted on them. Peacemakers have always sought to humanize each side to the other. Understanding leads to the possibility of empathy. Trust comes if people feel safe enough to interact and risk getting to know each other as individuals. Could the systemic approach be used to foster understanding and empathy between opposing groups? Could we resolve irreconcilable differences if we surfaced and appreciated the underlying dynamics that are unseen and unaddressed?

To explore these questions I facilitated a political constellation on the challenge of fostering peace between the Israelis and the Palestinians. The focus question was, *"How can the United States enhance its effectiveness in establishing peace between the Israelis and the Palestinians?"* While the historical roots of the conflict go back three millennia, American involvement started in the middle of the twentieth century after the British withdrawal from Palestine. Official efforts to broker peace started in earnest after the 1967 war. The high-water mark of those efforts was realized on September 17, 1978, by President Jimmy Carter when Menachem Begin and Anwar El Sadat signed a treaty between Israel and Egypt at Camp David. While there have been other successes, such as the establishment of the Palestinian Authority through the Oslo Accords in 1993 and 1995 and the initiation of the "two-state solution," a viable and lasting peace has yet to be realized.

Despite the American government's significant investments of time, talent, and billions of dollars in the region for close to half a century, peaceful coexistence in the Holy Land is still a dream.[1] Why should Americans keep trying, given the Sisyphean-like odds of success? 9/11 is one compelling reason. American diplomats in the Middle East have stated behind closed doors that the USA's fate is tied to the fate of the Palestinian people. As long as the conflict remains unresolved, the instability of a very unstable region will keep the USA and other parts of the globe at risk. Even a partial resolution of the conflict would reduce the threat to homeland security.

Eight participants attended the political constellation session to explore this issue. Most had limited experience as representatives. One other person besides myself had spent time in Israel or in the West Bank/Gaza area. Warm-up activities were conducted to help familiarize the participants with the energetic aspects of being in a state of conflict. Actual personal conflicts that participants were experiencing were constellated. The exercise underlined how the dynamic of conflict between individuals or groups is visceral and personal. Polarized feelings in a conflict show up as helpless or powerful and fearful or angry. These feelings are played out in projections around the archetypes of victim, perpetrator, and rescuer. When we are less caught up in our reactive judgments based on these archetypes, new possibilities can surface for reconciliation.

The group brainstormed twenty-five different "actors" involved in the Israeli-Palestinian conflict and narrowed the number down to the top eight, which included: Israeli settlers (Set); Israeli Palestinians (IP); Israelis (Jew); Palestinians in the West Bank and Gaza (Pal); holy sites sacred to Christian, Jewish, Islam, and other religions (SacS); the Holocaust (Hol); the American public (USA); and the international community (Inter). I reminded everyone that the Fatah party in the West Bank had a very different stance toward Israel than the Hamas party in Gaza did. Israel proper is also highly diverse. Hasidic Jews, for example, don't believe Israel has the right to be a country until the Messiah returns. For the sake of simplicity, the groups selected were those considered the most broadly representative. Each representative was handed a card with the name of one of the groups written on it, but I asked everyone to hold off looking at their cards. They found their places in the room and stood there with no agenda other than to notice what they noticed.

While still in the mode of a blind constellation, they were asked to report out. The representative for the *Israeli Palestinians* felt anxious and upset. Although the representative for the *Holocaust* felt a connection with the person behind her, she also felt heavy and detached. A few representatives circled up in the middle showing interest in each other while the *Israelis* and *Palestinians* watched in a detached manner from a distance.

The representatives arranged themselves as shown in Figure 14-1.

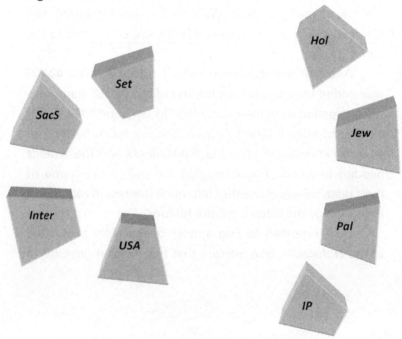

**Figure 14-1**

Another unnamed representative, the *solution,* was added to the constellation. She felt drawn to the *Palestinians* and moved to where she could stand beside the representative for them. Although she had not yet looked at her card, the *solution* felt that she was key to a positive outcome. I asked the group to notice if anything changed for them with the addition of the new, unnamed representative.

*USA* reported she felt attached to *Holocaust* and moved to her side. The *Israeli Palestinians* felt somewhat better and turned toward the others. The others looked thoughtful. I asked the representatives to look at their cards and tell the others who they were. While they were thinking about who they were, I told them the new representative was a *solution* that leads to peace. Surprisingly, the *solution* felt that the Israelis themselves should come to terms with the trauma of the Holocaust. With this acknowledgment, the *Holocaust* was able to turn and feel more connected to the entire group.

Another representative (who I referred to as 48/67) was added to represent the trauma of the Palestinians who were expelled from their homeland in 1948 and 1967. When 48/67 was added, *Israeli Palestinians* felt much better. The *solution* stated that both the *Palestinians* and the *Israelis* needed to see and acknowledge the pain and trauma of their past. However, neither felt much interest in relating to their own or the other's painful history.

USA reported feeling almost obsessively protective of the *Holocaust. She* realized that her fixation gave her a

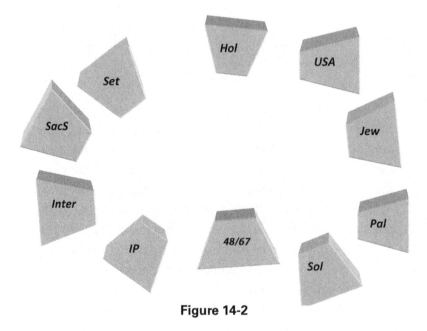

**Figure 14-2**

sense of moral superiority. As long as *she* held on to that payoff, she could not see the others, their sufferings, or the *solution*. The *solution* felt connected to the *Israelis, Palestinians,* and *Israeli Palestinians* and their respective traumas. As the dialogue unfolded, the representatives moved into the arrangement shown in Figure 14-2.

**Reflections:** Based on their experience in this constellation, the participants concluded that the shift needed to strengthen America's peacemaking was to let go of its sense of moral superiority. It was not exactly clear where this sense came from. Perhaps, as a result of its role in defeating Nazi Germany, it became the protector and rescuer of those who suffered from the Holocaust. Yet, until the American public was able to acknowledge and grieve the suffering of the oppressed people in its own history, it could not expect the Israelis and the Palestinians to acknowledge and grieve the suffering they have experienced and caused each other. This crucial step would lay the emotional and spiritual groundwork for peace. No one should claim the exclusive mantle of hero or victim or project the shadow of the perpetrator on others. The peace initiative hosted by President Carter in 1978 at Camp David was the last time an American government enabled a successful outcome. Since then, mediators from the Department of State have been searching in the wrong place for a solution. The place to look was not in Tel Aviv or Ramallah but in the American national psyche. If the USA faced more boldly its own national traumas and failings, it might gain an unspoken but essential level of credibility.

Apologies to the reader for the repetition, but there is no escaping the necessity to, in Mahatma Gandhi's message, "*Be the change that you wish to see in the world.*"

Another systemic obstacle may be a displacement

syndrome, which I discussed in chapter 7 ("The Sharks versus the Elephants"). This Middle East region of the world has been at war almost constantly for the entirety of recorded history. A huge amount of pain and suffering going back for many, many generations has been accumulated in the collective unconscious that influences the behavior of all the different groups and factions. Until that pain is acknowledged and the tragedies grieved and honored at some type of universal Wailing Wall, the violence is likely to continue to erupt from the collective unconsciousness of that region.

## The Roots of Racial Dynamics

The media was full of reports of rioting in the city of Baltimore sparked by the death of a young black man in police custody. I didn't have a crystal ball, but the workshop scheduled that month in Washington, DC, to explore the hidden dynamics of race suddenly became a timely topic. More than thirty people showed up; about a third were African-American; the rest were Caucasian and one woman from Afghanistan. Eight or nine people in the group were familiar with constellation work. Two people were from Baltimore and lived in the inner city.

After introductions we discussed why we had come that night. One Caucasian spoke about how people were dying and it was time to put a stop to it. An African-American woman objected that the term "people" was too generic. Young black men were being killed by police. The San Francisco police had killed her nephew over a two-dollar ticket. The tension in the room started to build. An African-American man spoke about the elephant of racism. No one talks about it yet it is there in our society and affecting his life. I replied we would be looking at that elephant but not with our verbal thinking mind. That part of our mind was prone to staying stuck in the same story based on judgments and preconceptions. If we used the nonverbal mind, the part that is present to "what is" in a quiet and open manner, we might assess a deeper, more felt-sense level of understanding.

I led the group through a paired exercise to demonstrate our subconscious connection with each other. Two volunteers stood a few feet apart. The one who was the issue holder touched the other person with the intention that she represented a challenging person in her life. The issue holder started to cry. I asked her to step back a few feet. She did and stopped crying. The representative who had been touched was looking down, impassive. I asked the issue holder to say to her, "I see you, and I agree to what is." Immediately there was a shift in the energy. The representative looked up at the issue holder. They both felt better and better about each other. The verbal mind, I explained to the group, holds on to the past or fears the future. Our nonverbal mind, however, is able to let go and be in the "now" that contains new insights and possibilities. Belief and experience continually reinforce each other. Switching to a nonverbal mode of thinking and experiencing is one way to break out of that continuous loop.

I further explained how trauma can be transgenerational. I had been in Israel over the New Year and attended a conference with Germans and Israelis. They had all been born after WWII yet still felt deeply burdened by the legacy of the Holocaust. Pain and guilt, anger and shame filled the room when that subject was raised. Confronting that pain and the victim-perpetrator dynamic that lived within them was overwhelming. Openly facing and discussing those intense feelings allowed a sense of wholeness and healing to emerge for both groups.

I asked for volunteers and gave each person that

stood up a card. Since we were doing a blind constellation I asked them not to look at their card and just trust the sensations and impulses they felt. This would keep us honest and preclude anyone from acting how they thought they were supposed to.

*Perpetrator, victim, observer,* and *rescuer* took their cards and found their places in the open space in the center of the room. Within a minute the man, a Caucasian, holding the victim card slowly went down to the floor reporting that he felt that he was being split open and eviscerated. The *rescuer* and *observer* moved closer to him. The *perpetrator* turned away and stared at the wall. I asked those sitting in their chairs who were not yet participating to keep breathing and stay with the tension and discomfort in the room. The *victim* may have felt bad but he was in control of what was happening and could withdraw as a representative if the experience became too intense. I asked others, if they felt inspired, to join the four representatives. One person joined the *perpetrator.* Three people joined the *victim:* one lying down beside him and two others standing close by. I handed each a card. One was *oppression and humiliation.* Another, *cultural expropriation.* The third, *exclusion.*

I kept extending the invitation to the group and others stepped in, taking the cards: *Africa, benefits* (from the slave system), *projecting shadow material onto others, heroes who advocated human rights, hidden payoff,* and *ancestors.* Finally, I asked the *perpetrators* to turn about and face the *victims.* They were unable to tell the *victims* that they saw them.

I put someone in to represent their *mother.* At first they were distant to each other. I asked the *mother* to tell the *perpetrators* she always had a place for them in her heart and would be there for them no matter what. Gradually, the *perpetrators* moved closer to their *mother.* They still looked confused, disorientated, and in pain. In a low voice, held by their *mother,* they were finally able to tell the victims that they saw them and their suffering. The victims reported they felt better, lighter, and more peaceful. "I did not know you were human," one of the *perpetrators* whispered. "They told me you weren't, but I see now you have feelings like me."

I called the participants who were still seated to come stand as a group where they could best see the constellation. They were representing *North American society.* "We see what happened and how you suffered," I asked them to say. "And we won't forget you and your suffering." I asked two young women in the group to represent the future. Maybe someday in the future this issue would be considered resolved and other concerns would be a priority. I asked them to tell the people caught up in the issue they would not forget them and their suffering, and to have faith that the future would be a better place.

Bringing the constellation to a close I asked the representatives who had joined the original four volunteers to look at their cards and share their experiences with the larger group. The feelings they felt and the impulses they had to move or say something were in alignment with the parts of the system they had been assigned. *Ancestors* had been just one person. She went back and forth between disdain for the *victims* and compassion and concern. My sense was she alternated between the different sets of ancestors and the radically different attitudes they possessed.

The representative for *the heroes who advocated human rights* said she was focused on and concerned about everyone, not just the victims. The woman who had been the mother smiled and added that Martin Luther King had said he was there not to just set the Negro free but to free everyone from the chains of prejudice. The woman whose nephew had been killed by police summarized what had taken place. She had once seen a cage where slaves were kept. Now she saw that everyone was in that cage no matter what role they played. Everyone was hurting and diminished in some way by slavery and its legacy.

In the closing circle people stood beaming at each other. They had been willing to experience something that was upsetting. Behavioral science tells us people are hardwired to seek pleasure and avoid pain. Yet the participants chose to go through this intense process. In return, they came away with a deeper insight into the dynamics of slavery and its impact on our society. Acknowledging what happened and agreeing to "what is" would not bring education and jobs to the inner cities. But it just might be a small step toward releasing the "frozen past" from the collective unconscious that underlies the social patterns of hopelessness and separation into two unequal societies. The constellation produced an image of a path that might lead to reconciliation. Replicating and strengthening that image so it becomes part of the collective consciousness could soften the hard edges that keep the races apart.[2]

# Chapter 15
# Professional Constellations

When life hands you a problem, you can try to change others or try to change yourself. Demanding that others change has about a zero percent success rate.

Trying to change yourself solely through mental analysis and willpower seldom works to the extent needed or desired. The constellation process may start with the mind, but then it goes much further, using the emotions and the physicality of the body to radically comprehend the issue. Physicality—sensations related to the emotions and the physical placement of representatives— offers a gateway to the subconscious—the ultimate arbitrator of any personal change. Past impressions, traumas, and disowned aspects of yourself are stored out of sight. Individual coping mechanisms, defenses, and denials keep them hidden but limit your ability to live life fully and effectively. Once the traumas are surfaced, seen, and attended to their disruptive energy can be released.

A person's disowned or forgotten parts, also hidden in the subconscious, are often wounded or incapacitated in some way. Once they are expressed and resourced they can return to a healthier state that supports life instead of hindering it.

## The Inner Dynamics of Success

About two-thirds of the constellations I've facilitated have been what I call "professional constellations." These constellations differ from those focused on groups and organizations because of the personal dimension. We can't escape the impact of our personal history on our professional activities and aspirations.

Although we might start with an organizational issue, the constellation becomes focused on the issue holder's professional aspirations. Frequently, the professional question or issue is found to have a direct link to something or someone in the person's family history. Paraphrasing the family therapist Virginia Satir (who was mentioned in previous chapters), what lingers from a person's past—be it unresolved or incomplete—can drive his or her seemingly irrational behavior in the present.[1] Since groups as well as individuals often display irrational behavior this principle is likely to hold true across the spectrum of human behavior.

A theme frequently raised during a professional constellation addresses the inner dynamics of success. If the goal is clear, then what is getting in the way of achieving it? Starting a business or changing careers are popular objectives. Mythologist Joseph Campbell famously advised young people to *"follow your bliss"* when making a life decision.[2] The piece he left out is that this is likely to be one of the scariest things you will ever do. One part of a person can have a clear and measurable objective in mind and a strong desire to achieve it. If the rest of the psyche is not aligned with that vision, however (especially when that lack of inner alignment is unconscious), the desired outcome will be frustratingly illusive. During a constellation, sensitive events from the past are sometimes unexpectedly uncovered. If I see one coming I always ask the issue holders if they wish to continue. They may not be ready for what is being revealed and should have a choice in the matter. The issue can be explored later in a more private setting if that is what they choose.

The case studies in this book are typical of the issues people bring to workshops, retreats, or individual coaching sessions. My job as the facilitator is to provide the participants with the opportunity to gain insights that arise from a shift in perspective. The issue holder's job is to use those insights, or at least allow them to touch the hidden parts of his or her essential self.

## Hidden Obstacle

Lee, a business coach, had worked with his client, a medical doctor, for several years. The MD was passionate about his vision for a holistic health center. With Lee's assistance, he mapped out a strategy and took a number of practical steps to turn his dream into a reality. To raise funds for the center's construction he approached a couple of financial providers. Naturally, they wanted to see a detailed business plan. Somehow the MD could never find the time to develop one. Lee tried a number of different ways to encourage his client to write the plan, but without success. He felt confused and frustrated. Why was the MD so resistant to doing what obviously had to be done? His attempts to discuss the issue went nowhere, and even generated some resentment. Hoping to gain some insight into this impasse, we set up a constellation as depicted in Figure 15-1.

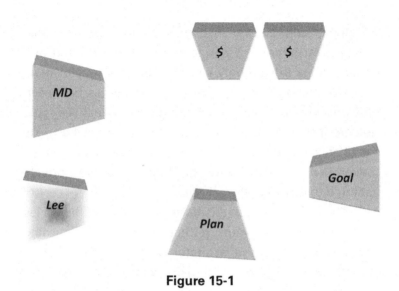

**Figure 15-1**

Because there was only one other person at the session in addition to Lee and me, we used pieces of paper to hold the space for parts of the constellation. In turn, I stood at each of the designated places and noticed what came to me. In the place for the MD, I felt that he was focused on his goal and did not notice the business plan or pay much attention to the sources of financing ($) that would fund it. I did find my right hand reaching out and trying to make contact with my coach. It was as if the MD was saying nonverbally, "Where are you? I need you beside me." Lee, who stood a step or two back, was also focused on the plan and the providers of the money. There seemed to be a "disconnect" between Lee and his client. The *goal,* or holistic health center, felt ready and waiting and a bit impatient with the lack of implementation. The *plan* could see his funding sources clearly and his *goal* from his peripheral vision, but did not have any connection or awareness of the MD or Lee.

I asked Lee if any of this made sense to him. He replied that the dynamics were intriguing in a tone that implied this self-observation was taking him out of his comfort zone. I invited Lee to stand in the different places as I had done and notice what he noticed as a representative. At the place of the goal, Lee was outspoken and forceful about his importance. From the place of the MD, he was vehement about needing his coach to work with him and wondering where he was. From his own place of the coach, Lee did not seem able to look at his client and stayed a step back behind him and to the side. His focus was still toward the *plan* and the *sources of financing.*

I asked the other participant at the meeting to represent the MD. He asked Lee if he was willing to accept his decisions about the health center and how to achieve it. Before he answered that question, I asked Lee, "Will you speak your truth to your client without holding back from fear of rejection or confrontation?" Lee answered, "Yes." Turning to face the MD, Lee affirmed that he would work with him without any attachment to his own agenda. I moved the participant into another space without saying who or what he represented. I shifted Lee back to the position of the MD and asked him whether he knew who or what the other person might be representing. Lee suggested that from the vantage point of the MD the new representative was the hidden payoff for not writing a successful business plan.

When I asked who or what the payoff was, Lee, as the MD, responded, "That is my spouse, and I am afraid I'll lose her if I go for my dream." After this insight surfaced I brought the constellation to an end. We had no mandate to explore the personal relationship of the MD with his spouse. They would need to have a frank discussion or consider counseling to resolve this issue. Lee left with an insight that could benefit his client. However, in the ensuing conversations with the MD, it became clear that he did not want to explore how his marriage was impacting his business goals. Lee eventually came to terms with this and the continued lack of progress. They amicably ended their coaching relationship.

## Survival Mode

One precept of the mythopoetic hero is "your wound is your gift." Redemption in the hero's journey, described by Joseph Campbell in *The Hero with a Thousand Faces,* comes to those brave enough to face that wound and accept with humility the lessons it teaches.[3] Sometimes that wound, according to systemic thinking, is not personally ours but part of our family system, as the following case study illustrates.

A human resources executive for a large international organization felt overwhelmed by the challenges he faced. A new president, responding to a radically shifting business environment, was dramatically changing his organization's structure and headcount. Starting with senior leadership on down, everyone at some point would be reapplying for their jobs. A significant number of management and staff would not be rehired. The words the executive used to describe the situation and how people felt included stressed, survival, uncertainty, devalued, chaos, identity, and rumors. The question for him was how to be calm, reassuring, and resourceful to his internal clients when his own reaction to the situation was an overwhelming sense of panic and helplessness.

To uncover the answer to his question, I started the constellation with three representatives: the *executive,* the *change* his international organization was going through, and the *reaction of staff* to this reorganization. A fourth representative was added that was the *source* of the feelings overwhelming the executive. The HR executive positioned the selected representatives as illustrated in Figure 15-2.

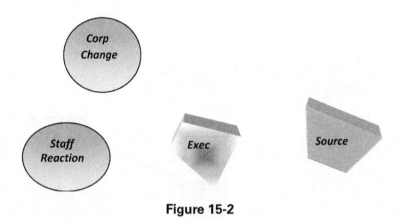

**Figure 15-2**

The *executive* was drawn to the *corporate change* and the *staff reaction* to the change. This is shown in the figure by how *he* is facing them and *his* close proximity. It is significant that the *source* of his angst about the change was facing away. The *staff reaction* reported feeling weak and confused. The *executive* also felt weak and unable to do more than look at them. The *source* reported being present as a witness but did not feel personally involved. I asked the executive about his own family history. Had there been something comparable in his family's past where people felt that their survival was at stake and there was uncertainty about the outcome? He came from a country that had been devastated by WWII. How badly had his family been affected? Since his immediate relatives had not served in the military, he thought at first they had not been adversely affected. But he remembered stories of his grandparents leaving their city to escape the bombing and find food in the countryside.

Scarcity of food and shelter, lack of essential services, uncertainties of how they would live all added up to a struggle for survival. I went back to the representative for *source* and changed who he stood for. The *source* was now

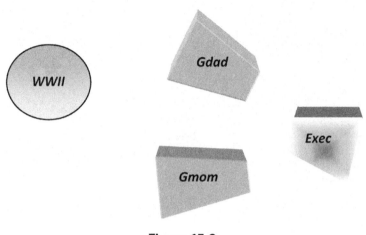

**Figure 15-3**

*WWII* and the adversity and uncertainties of that time. The *staff reaction* and *corporate change* were now his *grandparents,* who went through those deprivations.

The executive was asked to stand in his place and honor his grandparents and other relatives and what they had been through. They had shown resourcefulness and had persevered. If they had not, he would not be standing here now. Their victory was his life. Their resourcefulness and resilience were a part of him. In gratitude, he would serve others who also faced a survival situation.

To affirm this connection his grandparents stood behind him (see Figure 15-3). Facing the *staff* who were caught up in reorganization the executive now felt calmer and more capable. I gave him a pad of blue sticky notes to represent his new sense of calmness and capacity. Taking notes off the pad he handed them out to staff as a gesture of his commitment and support. He would draw strength from his family system and his clients could draw strength from him.

**Reflections:** The HR executive, like everyone else, can't help but make use of his "self" at the workplace. The parts of that self that are unconscious are more vulnerable to the vicissitudes of life. To paraphrase the oft-quoted words from Ralph Waldo Emerson's "Ode to William H. Channing," your unconscious stuff is in the saddle and rides you. Ironically, those wounds, hidden in the subconscious, can also be a source of strength when they are brought to awareness in a way that honors the past. The challenges were still there, but now the executive had more access to the resourcefulness within himself and his family system.

## Empowerment Angel

Ned, a senior manager with a global organization, felt that he was selling himself short in meetings with his peers. Some nebulous fear held him back from asserting himself in a constructive manner. He worried he was showing up as too passive. He knew he could do better, yet somehow the dynamic part of his personality seemed to hide when he most needed it. It was time to make a change in his job assignment, but he found himself waiting for others to offer him his next position. Two representatives were chosen: one for the dynamic and empowered self that felt competent, proactive, and influential; the other for the self that was playing small and holding back. I asked Ned to describe those two parts of himself.

The first was present when he was skiing in the mountains. He felt generous and connected with himself and others. He gave fully without attachment to help others develop their skills. The second one reminded him of his father. He had kept a low profile throughout his work life, avoiding the limelight and the conflicts that arise when a person asserts himself. Ned's relationship with his father was good in that he always felt supported and appreciated. Yet he believed his father had traded making a difference

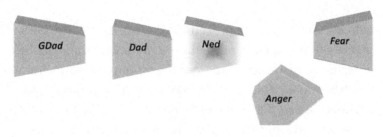

**Figure 15-4**

for the security that anonymity seemed to offer.

As shown in Figure 15-4, representatives for his father and grandfather lined up behind Ned. Feeling the flow of their support Ned faced a representative for the fear that was holding him back. Something seemed to melt in his chest as he looked at the fear. "Does the fear represent loyalty to your father?" I asked. "Do you fear the loss of your father's love and approval if the dynamic side of yourself takes over?"

Ned then stepped out of the constellation and a representative took his place. Suddenly, Ned acted out a part of himself that thought it should scold him for playing small. When I asked who also treated him that way, Ned replied that his wife did. This was his atonement for letting himself and others down. I suggested to Ned that there were healthier and more effective ways than raging at himself to be the person he wanted to be. I asked Ned to step back in the lineup, face his *father,* and thank him for the gift of life.

To resolve a possible entanglement, Ned honored his father's fate and asked him to look kindly on him as he lived his own life. Ned also acknowledged his *grandfather* who was beaming at him. The *grandfather,* who had lived a successful and influential life, said he felt like Ned's birth angel, here to be an infinite source of selfless, creative energy that Ned could draw upon to fulfill his mission. The participants stood around the *grandfather/birth angel* and took in the wonderful blessing energy he seemed to radiate. It was one of those transcendent moments that nourished and touched everyone in the room. After the session and before we left for the evening, the group sat quietly for a few minutes to soak in that peaceful and nourishing field of energy.

**Reflections:** Consciously connecting with one's lineage can be a source of strength. The anger and disappointment being expressed by Ned and his wife toward himself may have been a form of atonement for events that occurred before he was born. By accepting the blessing from his lineage, Ned untangled himself from the past. In return, he gained a felt-sense of living his own life that was a boon to all the participants in the room. Another part of Ned's self-imposed limitation could have been his unconscious loyalty to his father. In truth, this misguided loyalty served no one. The best way to honor his father was to live his own life even if that meant being more successful than his father had been. Constellations reveal that the departed want their descendants to be happy and to do something good with their lives. They neither need nor want this needless form of sacrifice based on a blind loyalty.

## Marketing Plan

Flor is a businesswoman who had set a goal for herself to have 60 percent of her days billable to her clients. The rest would be her free time to do as she wanted. Her problem was she been doing everything but the marketing needed to achieve her objective. She knew what she wanted and how to get it, so what was keeping her stuck? Representatives were chosen and set up, as shown in Figure 15-5, for herself, her business goal, her marketing activities (Mkt), and the distractions (Distract) that she

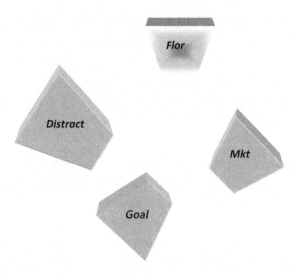

**Figure 15-5**

focused on instead of marketing.

After the representatives had some time to settle into the field, I walked around them. I noticed something and called Flor over to where I stood. When I pointed out to her that there was very little energy in the constellation, her comments were analytical instead of somatic at first, and she agreed. The representatives also agreed, although *distractions* said he was very important and implied that he was the most potent part of all.

An unnamed representative was placed to the side. *Distractions* pointed to her. She was significant to him. I asked Flor if she was willing to explore her family issues and explained that this could turn emotional. She expressed her willingness so I talked about how a person's business success can be affected by the health of the parent and child relationship. Recall from chapter 6 ("The Orders of Organizations") that the family therapist Bert Hellinger speaks of this as the extent to which the issue holder takes her mother as her mother despite the deficits she may have experienced in being mothered. Was Flor willing to look at her relationship with her mother? She answered that she was, so time was spent on healing phases and movements with the representatives of the mother and grandmother in her maternal lineage. Tears and hugs followed. *Flor's mother* and grandmother stood behind the business and faced Flor's goal and the *distractions* and *marketing activities* in between them. Her *goal* started withdrawing until it was nearly out of the room. Her *distractions* joined her at her side as if they were her ally.

This reminded me of a common therapeutic saying: *"The parts of yourself that you reject will turn against you."*[4] Flor accepted those parts of herself and believed they could help her if given the right place in her life. She moved to join *marketing,* but *marketing* did not feel ready to join with her. Since the *goal* had withdrawn, what really was her true heart's desire? A representative was chosen and placed in the constellation. *Marketing* felt drawn to the *heart's desire* and stood next to her. Flor now felt free to join with both of them and they smiled, laughed with delight, and hugged each other. Unlike at the beginning of the constellation, the energy was now vibrant and alive.

**Reflections:** I did not press Flor to reveal her heart's desire at the end of the constellation. She had gone into a deeply emotional place. My sense was she would need to take her time to integrate those feelings before discussing with a trusted friend what she really wanted to do with her life and what that might put at risk. She had bravely faced the hidden truth that what she thought she wanted and what she actually wanted were different. Being honest with oneself is the difficult first step in breaking free from the inner constraints that keep a person from living life with energetic fullness.

### The Lady or the Tiger

An IT specialist, Max was recognized by his employer for his technical skills. Three times over the previous nine years, however, he had gotten tired of the difficult, sometimes abusive, working environment and quit. Twice before, after a few months, the organization persuaded him to come back. This time, to lure him back, they were offering a unique arrangement where he could work part of the year in San Francisco, a city that he loved. He felt that he should find a healthier place to work, but it was hard to say no to that kind of flexibility. Could he find it within himself to move on? With his exceptional IT talents he would always find a good job, yet there was a fear that kept him hostage to this unhealthy workplace. Where did it come from?

Max set up the constellation shown in Figure 15-6: himself, the healthy workplace he wanted to work in, and his fear, which encompassed all the parts of his dilemma.

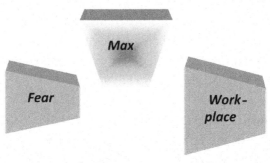

**Figure 15-6**

As Max observed the dynamic between the three representatives, he related that he was estranged from his father. Even though they lived in the same city, he did not see him or the rest of his family. He felt that his father had been abusive toward him when he was a child.

I remarked that that which you run away from, you also run toward. There might be a connection between Max not being able to leave a work environment and leaving a

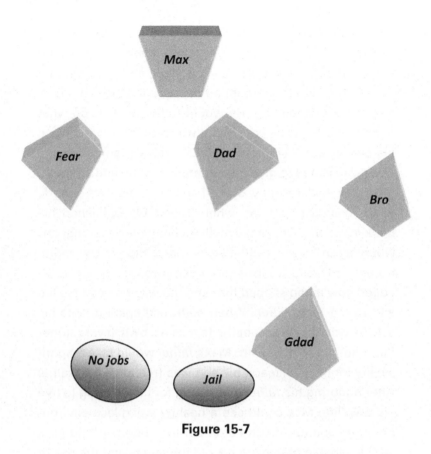

**Figure 15-7**

parent, both of which were emotionally unhealthy. Life is paradoxical, and paradoxically, the way to freedom was in returning to his relationship with his father. What had happened to his father? Had he suffered trauma growing up?

Max's father turned out to have been through a lot. Objects were placed behind his representative (see Figure 15-7) to represent his history, which included jail time, a brother who died young, scarcity of jobs during the Great Depression, and a difficult relationship with his own father. Max took the place of his representative. He was asked to tell his *father*, "I see you and I see what you went through" and "I didn't understand what you went through, but now

I do." Max was asked to acknowledge to his *father* the fear that kept him from leaving his job. Max's *father* did not want to look at or acknowledge the son's fear, and he would not turn around and face *what had happened* in his own life. It was too overwhelming. He would rather tell his son what to do and pretend he knew what was best for him than face his own fears. A supportive force in Max's family lineage was represented to give the father inspiration and strength.

Max had recently started mythopoetic men's work, which gained popularity when Robert Bly published his book *Iron John*. One of the mythopoetic concepts is that our wounds can give us a gift if we embrace them. Max's *father* turned and faced what he had been through. He acknowledged how it had shaped him and the way he lived his life and raised his children. When *he* turned again to face his son, he was able to accept the fear as his own. It was something he had to deal with. Max's *father* would take responsibility for his own fears; his son was free to do the same. After honoring his *father* and asking for his blessing to live his own life, Max could see a healthy workplace environment in his future. With his *father* in support behind him, he felt capable of leaving his old job and taking the risk of finding something better.

**Reflections:** We like to think we can put a fire wall between work life and personal life, but it's all indivisibly one life. Our dilemmas and the answers to them span both realms. Confronting the systemic effects of past traumas is the price tag for the freedom to more fully live one's own life.

### Gaining Confidence

A business professional with fifteen years of work experience, Jan wanted to develop a better "elevator" speech because when she was in front of a potential client, her marketing pitch was not having the desired effect. Something was missing. During our initial discussion, it became clear that the missing piece was not *what* she was saying to her potential clients but *how* she was saying it. Her nonverbal expressions were not communicating the kind of quiet confidence that others sense and respond to. First impressions take place in a flash. How could Jan give an impression of the competence and creditability that was who she was?

A representative was selected to be a potential client. Jan stood in front of her and gave her elevator speech. After the half-minute presentation, the *client* was asked about her impression. Though it was not unfavorable, the *client* did not feel energized or engaged. Jan picked an older man to represent her competent, confident self and he went and

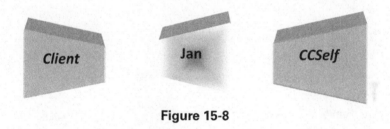

Figure 15-8

stood behind her, as depicted in Figure 15-8.

Although there was some reaction from others that she should have picked a woman, I pointed out that we all have both a female and a male aspect within us. Carl Jung called this opposite gender the anima for men and the animus for women. Female leaders like Margaret Thatcher were certainly in touch with their animus. Male leaders like Abraham Lincoln were not afraid to draw upon their anima. Jan stood for a while facing her *client* and then repeated her speech. The *client* reported that she felt more receptive. Jan also felt more capable and confident. However, the *client* wondered to what extent Jan felt "safety in numbers." Was it possible that her positive reaction might be directed more toward the *confident, competent self* who stood beside Jan? Jan picked representatives for her education, work experience, family and friends, values, and

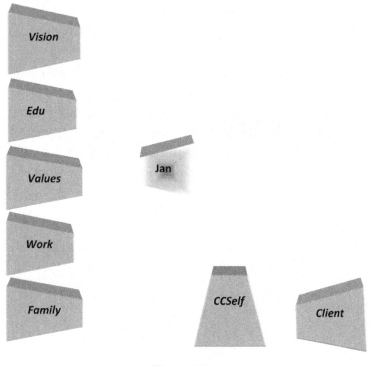

**Figure 15-9**

vision. They formed a line, as shown in Figure 15-9.

Jan moved slowly from one representative to the next. She expressed gratitude to each part of her life for all it had given her. Hugs were exchanged. They knew who she was and what she had and would achieve. They would always be there for her whenever she needed them. They believed in her and her ability to change the world for the better. At the end of the line Jan greeted her *confident, competent self. "All of this,"* she pointed to the line behind her, "has made you who you are. You are always with me to help me do my work." Some parts voiced their encouragement. Others smiled in approval.

Jan embraced her *confident, competent self* and turned to face her *client.* She introduced this part of herself to her client and affirmed she would have the qualities it represented to draw upon. The *client* was impressed but still unconvinced. "When he is not there, can I rely upon you?" the *client* asked Jan. The *confident, competent* self stepped off to the side. Jan looked at her *client* and gestured toward her lineup of the aspects of her life. "You can trust me to bring all that I am to the work I do." The *client* nodded and smiled. "This time" the *client* told the group, "I believe Jan."

**Reflections:** Whether they know it or not, people have a number of inner resources. Staying connected to those resources energetically provides a wellspring of confidence. People who believe in you and wish you well, achievements that demonstrate your capabilities, those who see you in a positive light all help mold the inner sense of self. The road to being "affirmed" by others is learning to be self-affirming and to remember the felt-sense of who you are.

## Website Mystery

Lila ran a small professional services company. She was concerned that she never seemed to find the time or motivation to set up a website. There were occasional slow times when she worried she was not doing enough to promote her services. Money was not the issue because she had two skilled webmasters in her extended family who had offered their services. Even so, she could not overcome some unexplained resistance to setting up a website despite the benefits it offered.

Lila selected three representatives for her constellation: the *website,* the part of her that said *"Yes"* to it, and the part of her that said *"No."* Lila positioned the representatives as shown in Figure 15-10.

**Figure 15-10**

The *Yes* part and the *website* seemed to delight in each other's company. The *website* reported that she felt like a small child who asks the No part, *"Why don't you like me?"* The *No* felt drawn to something else. She could not say just what that something else was, but it felt encompassing to her. Lila took the place of her *No* representative. Another representative was placed in front of her where she had been looking so attentively. Was this a case of divided loyalty? What would she be saying *No* to if she said *Yes* to the website? Clearly, Lila was saying Yes to a mysterious something in front of her. It had a big draw upon her.

Lila quietly faced the unknown figure. (See the new configuration in Figure 15-11.) After a short time, she bowed and then prostrated to it. It was the sacred part of her life. For most of her adulthood her spiritual practices and beliefs had been central to her life and relationships. She honored this part of herself and the place that it would always have in her heart. She asked that it bless her and look kindly on her work in the business world. For a long minute she opened up to the energy of that blessing, visibly receiving and taking in. Then, turning, she faced the *website* and the

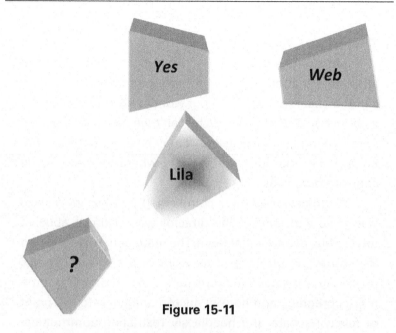

**Figure 15-11**

*Yes* with her *spiritual life* standing close by. "Do you feel inspired to move toward them?" I asked. No, she wanted them to come to her and they did so joyfully. Lila moved to the center and stood there supported by *Yes*. The website had now become her *business life*. With a long, meaningful look she said Yes to both.

**Reflections:** The conflict between being spiritual versus being in business goes back to the archetypical question of serving God or Mammon delineated by the biblical prophets. Ancient archetypes can touch and shape our values even if we don't actively ascribe to them or even think about them. An unexamined polarity can keep a person within the restrictions of an "either/or" when in actuality the open space of a "yes/and" is just as valid. A few months later, Lila started a new venture with her partner that focused on developing "Enlightened Leadership." The details of this venture became the focus of her new website.

### The Fog of War

More often than you would expect, office conflicts arise over matters that seem hardly worth the fight. The curious observer can't help but wonder what is driving the dysfunctional behaviors. "Why can't we all get along?" as Rodney King famously asked. It may be a cocreated world, but we can only look for answers where we have some control—ourselves.

A professional, Alice complained that her workplace was toxic and fearful. The director was at times abusive toward his management team. The management team tried to keep a low profile and stay out of the director's way. Lately, Alice believed the director's behaviors had become more egregious and he was micromanaging—to the point of falsifying data and needlessly restricting communication. Alice's supervisor did not want his staff to tell him too much so he had plausible deniability. While Alice was not directly in the "line of fire," she nonetheless felt that she was wandering in a fog tense with unseen danger. She had held only two jobs during her career. The previous one had been even more difficult. She had finally left it when the stress became overwhelming.

When asked about her goal for this session, Alice cited more compassion. She could not change her leaders, so she had found a way to be more detached through centering prayer. It was interesting that both work environments throughout her career had been toxic. I asked about her family life. This fog she talked about sounded like the fog of war. Who had been through a war? She recounted that her parents had emigrated from Serbia, but neither had been directly involved in WWII. Her father's father had left his family behind and moved to South Africa. Reportedly, he never made enough money to bring his family there or return to visit. Representatives were picked for the grandfather, South Africa and Serbia. As Alice set up them up (see Figure 15-12), she felt a lot of anxiety, so a representative was added for fear.

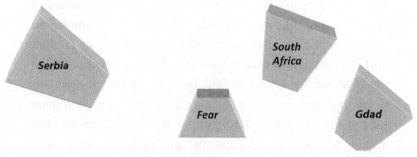

**Figure 15-12**

The constellation revealed that the *grandfather* did not feel connected to *Serbia* or *South Africa*. He was a man without a country. Ironically, *South Africa* looked favorably upon him. *South Africa* seemed interested in the fear, but also adverse to it. Whatever the fear or anxiety was about, it somehow kept him stuck in his no-man's-land. An object was placed to the right of fear to represent its source or cause. Alice felt very weird when this *source* was brought in. Something had happened. People in her family had died, perhaps others too. There seemed to be family secrets that drove her grandfather to leave. His brothers had left also, and the one she knew about had not prospered either.

Her *grandfather* lay down. He had died a number of years ago. Alice went to his side and grieved his passing and his difficult life. She thanked him for his sacrifice and honored his search for a better life. She took a jacket and used it as a shroud to cover him and acknowledge his passage to the other world. Alice left her *grandfather* and went up to *Serbia,* who had been watching silently. She acknowledged her roots in the region. She would always remember where her family came from. *Serbia* smiled upon her and they embraced. A sense of peace and completion touched Alice and all the participants in the room.

A few months later, Alice returned for another constellation. She still felt that her organization was toxic and stressful, and this was affecting her health. I remembered her connection to Serbia and the long history of conflict and devastation it was known for. We had acknowledged the grandfather who had left, but what about those who never had the chance to leave? I set up representatives for the toxic fog that characterized her workplace and the source of that fog. The source quickly grew weary and lay down. The burden he was carrying was overwhelming desolation. I added two other representatives to help him contain that sense of being overwhelmed. They lay down as well. I asked Alice to look at those representatives and acknowledge the terrible experiences they had lived through and perhaps had died from. It was possible they represented her ancestors whom she identified with in some way. Alice honored their fate and promised them she would do something good with her life in memory of them. The representatives reported that being seen by Alice gave them a peaceful feeling and the constellation was brought to a close.

**Reflections:** Many people in the Americas have ancestors who left the "old" country for a better life in the New World. They felt forced to leave because of war and oppression. For the most part, they and their descendants found a better life. Yet many constellations reveal that what happened in the old country came with them. If you fail to acknowledge your family history, in some strange way you relive it or it lives on through you. Ignorance of one's family history does not give you a free pass. Remembering and honoring the lives of previous generations strengthens the freedom to live one's own life without reenacting the traumas of the past. The insights Alice gained helped her face the office dramas with more objectivity and compassion. She stayed with her organization but was better able to insulate herself from the collective stress in the environment.

## Staffing Disaster

Seth founded his company nearly thirty years ago. Over that time he had hired more than two hundred people. To his disappointment, however, none of them had turned out to be high performers. In his words, they had, without exception, been mediocre in the jobs he had hired them for. "So why," I asked, "did you consistently, over such a long period of time, make such poor choices or have such bad luck choosing employees?" Looking forward, the most important question was how could he do a better job hiring staff.

Representatives were chosen for Seth, the job candidate who would prove to be a high performer, and the job candidate who would turn out to be mediocre. Seth positioned the mediocre candidate in between himself and the high performer. When asked why he set up the representatives in that configuration, Seth stated that the mediocre candidates were coming between him and the type of candidates he wanted to hire. While this was a snapshot of the current situation, it seemed too focused on the problem to lead to a solution. I reset the constellation as shown in Figure 15-13.

The identity of "A" and "B," the two job candidates in front of the businessman, were not revealed. One was the high performer and one was mediocre; only I knew which one was which.

Seth's representative was not drawn to either A or B. He looked instead at a spot in front of them. A participant

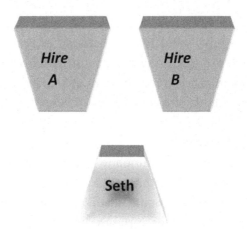

**Figure 15-13**

was asked to sit on that spot. She did not look at the *candidates* or *Seth,* but in another direction. A representative for Seth's country of origin, China, was placed there. Seth took his place in the constellation. China gazed serenely at Seth and the person on the ground in front of him. (See Figure 15-14.)

"Was there something about leaving China when you were a young man that was traumatic?" I asked Seth. He nodded yes but was reluctant to discuss what happened. A representative was placed next to *China* as the people involved in that trauma. I tried several different sentences to see which one described the connection between what had happened in China and the issue around hiring new staff. After several tries, *China* suggested the word *"atonement."* The word resonated in the room as if someone had rung a bell. "Tell the people in China you are sorry for what happened, and your atonement has been to hire the wrong people for jobs at your company," I suggested. As soon as Seth's representative said the sentence, the tension in the room eased.

The real Seth, sitting nearby, reported that he felt

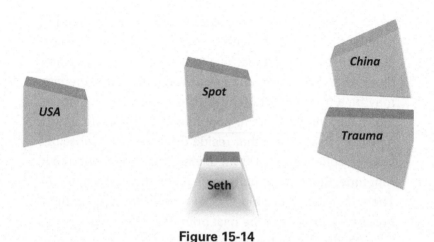

**Figure 15-14**

great. Some kind of burden had been lifted. A representative for the United States was placed in the constellation across from where *China* stood. "Introduce China and the people you left behind to your new country. Although you are an American now, let them know you will always have a place for them in your heart." When this was done, the high-performance candidate reported that she could see the businessman more clearly.

**Reflections:** As the constellation came to a close, I reminded Seth, "At some point when you are ready, you will need to talk about the trauma to a confidant and determine whether or how you should make amends to the people in your past." A conscious act of atonement has a limited time span. Unconscious acts can encompass a lifetime.

## Resolving Workplace Conflict

Conflict at work is inevitable, but this is not as grim as it sounds. Debating different views improves decision-making and creativity. It's when differences become personalized and others are denigrated or silenced that the

costs add up. At my constellation workshops the participants often want help with a workplace conflict. The constellation usually reveals an unresolved family dynamic
that needs to be seen and acknowledged. That something
may be a trauma or tragedy whose impact is still resonat-
ing in the family system, sometimes many years after it
occurred. Past events that reside deep in the unconscious
keep people in conflict from seeing their opponent in current time. Clear the grip of the past and their eyes open up.
Thereafter they can rationally deal with the issue without
projecting images of the past onto their opponent.

It's likely you have a person at work you regard as
high maintenance or even toxic. If you are generous you
might declare this to be a personality conflict, but you still
avoid interacting. It takes a lot to forgo the temptation to
blame the "toxic" person and investigate your side of the
uncomfortable tensions. Who or what does this person,
your reaction to him, and the dynamics between you represent in your own personal history? The answers may bring
up difficult, even painful, emotions rooted in the past. That
discomfort was the reason the answers resided below the
threshold of awareness. Bringing the past to awareness and
giving it space in the present allows the emotional charge
it carries to be resolved. From this perspective the difficult
person in your life is actually an ally instead of an irritation. An ally impels you to look at and integrate unacknowledged or disowned parts long banished to some emotional
basement. When those parts are welcomed home, stifled
energy is freed up to fuel new possibilities. Ironically, that
difficult person may seem to change and become easier to
deal with. More likely, you have changed and are no longer
so affected by certain behaviors that activated hidden psychological wounds.

## The Hidden Sources of Conflict

Sam, a manager in a high-tech company, was experiencing a conflict at work with another manager. Their two units needed to work together, so the conflict could not be ignored or written off as just a difference in personal styles. Sam felt that the other manager was treating him unfairly. He believed he had tried to work things out in a professional manner in good faith but was being rebuffed. He was at a loss over what he had done to warrant the other manager's hostility and distrust. The fact that he was Jewish and the other person was African-American somehow added to their communication problems.

While going into the details of the conflict, Sam mentioned that his father had survived the Holocaust as a slave laborer. His immediate family all perished in the gas chambers. After the war, he emigrated to America and eventually opened a store in a rough Chicago neighborhood. His store was robbed several times, and he suffered physically and financially. Sam shed tears as he related what his father had been through. I suggested that the abuse and trauma in his father's life was connected to the conflict Sam was dealing with in his workplace.

A victim-perpetrator dynamic may have become part of his family system and continued to reenact itself. Representatives were chosen for Jewish victims and Nazi perpetrators and set up facing each other from a safe distance. (See Figure 15-15.) They were not told at first who or what they represented.

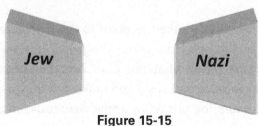

**Figure 15-15**

The *Jewish* victim felt fearful. The *Nazi* perpetrator felt curious about the person he was looking at yet also detached. Sam gave more details about his father, who struggled with rage and alcoholism. The representatives of this dynamic were moved to the background, and representatives for Sam and his father were selected and placed in the foreground (as shown in Figure 15-16).

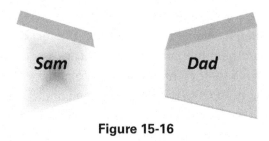

**Figure 15-16**

Another victim and perpetrator were also placed into the constellation as part of his father's story, as shown in Figure 15-17.

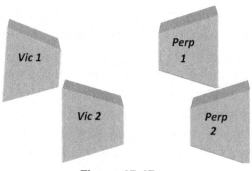

**Figure 15-17**

The *father* was asked to point to the *first perpetrator* and then to the *second victim,* who lay on the floor, and say to his son, "Look what they did!" And then point to the *second perpetrator* and say, "And look what they are doing now!" After hearing this a few times, Sam took his place as his own representative and replied to his *father, "I see what they did. It was not right. I understand your pain and rage."* The *father* visibly calmed down. The person who had this role related later that the experience of representing Sam's father was meaningful in his own personal work. (This phenomenon of finding an unexpected connection with the person you are representing is fairly common.)

Sam honored his father and his fate and said to him, "Please look kindly on me as I live my own life." *Mothers* were placed behind the *perpetrators* to help soften and open their hearts. *The perpetrators* became weaker and lay down on the floor. *The perpetrators* told their victims that it was not personal; their actions were part of the times. Sam was asked to stand on a stage where he could overlook the dynamics that had shaped his life. From the perspective of his higher self, he knew what he was taking on when he was born into his family. It takes courage for the children of Holocaust survivors to confront the legacy of its terrible brutality. I asked Sam if he could agree to "what is." I told him that hate, judgment, and resistance would keep him and his family stuck in the past. Looking at the representation of what his family had been through, Sam spread his arms and said, "I agree to it. I agree to all of it."

**Reflections:** Agreeing to "what is" is not an act of forgiveness or reconciliation toward the perpetrators. Their own dignity and personal growth requires them to take responsibility and be accountable for their actions. If they are able to grieve with their victims over what occurred a healing is possible for both. Sam initiated his healing process by acknowledging a terrible reality and its impact. Seeing the horror of the past paradoxically enabled him to see a different future. Acknowledging and feeling the pain in his family system helped his subconscious make the distinction between what was his to carry and what he could leave with his parents' generation. A person's outer condition reflects his or her inner condition even when those conditions were buried somewhere in the subconscious. Recapitulating old traumas will be emotionally intense. Yet, it can help free a person from being entangled in the fate of others and release energy that has been trapped in the family system.

## The Bear and the Jackal

Bill told me he was feeling confused and depressed about his work and personal life. As the CEO of a visible and well-regarded firm, he spent much of his time jetting around the globe negotiating deals between international clients and partners. Like most high-powered professionals, his identity and his work were closely bound together. As exciting, meaningful, and absorbing as his work life had been, it was time to make a change. He was uncertain about what was next. Many of his closest friends and associates were retired or preparing to make that move. This had encouraged him to begin transition planning with an HR consultant. His retirement was well funded. Yet, he felt ambivalent. Some friends and family were in failing health. He was in his mid-sixties, but slowing down seemed like a death sentence. Why voluntarily join the camp of those who might be making their final transition sooner rather than later? If he was not a high-profile CEO who was he?

A constellation was set up with three representatives: his work life, himself, and his personal life. Bill's *work life* reported it was focused and feeling strong and confident.

The representative for Bill felt restricted and even bound in some way that limited his mobility. His *personal life* felt ignored and sad. It was missing out. *Personal life* moved closer to Bill and then back a few steps. *Personal life* did not like the distance between it and Bill, but standing closer did not bring any sense of relief either. Following their impulse to move, the representatives ended up as shown in Figure 15-18.

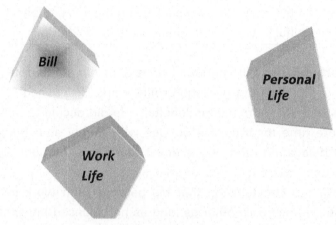

**Figure 15-18**

*Personal life* felt more engaged by Bill but did not trust his intentions. *Work life* reported it was trying to come between Bill and *his personal life;* not to get it out of the way but to fill it with competence and passion. At this point Bill took his place in the constellation. He acknowledged the fear and ambivalence he felt toward his personal life. Work life was seen as a place of eternal youth and purpose, while personal life seemed the exact opposite. Two other representatives were placed slightly behind and to the side of personal life to represent friends and family. Was Bill ready to be available to them?

*Personal life* asked Bill, "Why does it have to be an either/or decision? Why can't you have both your personal life and your work life?" Bill was asked to find the place in himself that was integrated and whole and speak his piece to *his personal life* and *his friends and family* about his intentions. "You are what really matters. I will bring my gifts from work into my personal life." This place of wholeness had the energy of a personal totem, and Bill's totem was a bear. The jackal was his shadow totem—the part of him that believed his personal life would never measure up compared to his work life. The bear trusted that his personal life would fulfill him and give him a place in the world.

**Reflections:** Bill continued to stay in his globe-trotting CEO job persuing his high-profile work. He pushed back his date for retirement indefinitely. He did decide to make more time for trips and outings with family and friends by delegating more to his direct reports. Retirement was something he would ease into instead of jump. He took from the constellation that his personal and work lives could enrich each other as long as he balanced his attention to both. Just attending more to his personal life was to him a form of semiretirement. Bill was by nature a type-A striver. Until he could see what he could achieve in his personal life that would give him comparable satisfaction, he was not about to let go of his high-flying day job. I suspected that Bill's opportunity for growth was more in his personal life than he might realize. His good health and supportive family enabled him to postpone taking that leap into the unknown. At some point, however, Bill would have to face his fear and take that leap. This would be easier if he followed the path of his bear totem; trusting his personal life and the place it offered him in the world. Building that trust would require uncovering and challenging the hidden beliefs and assumptions, the jackal part of his psyche that fueled his fear of letting go.

# Chapter 16
# The Search for Success

**W**hen it comes to success, why do some people seem to have the Midas touch? Two people with comparable ability, motivation, and background not infrequently achieve radically different levels of success. According to systemic thinking, intangible reasons can dramatically tilt the playing field. These intangibles are rooted in a person's subconscious, which retains impressions of one's past and the influences of previous generations. As I mentioned briefly in chapter 4 ("Third Pillar: The Knowing Field"), epigenetic research indicates that environmental trauma can affect subsequent generations even though none of the descendants were exposed to the original trauma.[1] As a professional constellation unfolds, it frequently becomes clear that the dysfunction in the person's work system mirrors the dysfunction in his family system.

In a sense, people show up at the workplace predisposed to experience a certain set of difficulties. Moving to another workplace might provide a temporary fix, but that won't keep the issue from replicating itself. The names of the actors change, but the same drama unfolds. A triggering event in the workplace that seems so emotionally overwhelming is often linked to an unresolved issue from the past. Acknowledging that issue and being fully present with it can turn the weakness into a source of learning and wisdom.

You may have a friend, as I do, whom you talk to about once a year. The circumstances change from year to year, but the basic storyline does not. His current boss and coworkers, just like the last ones, have something against him. No matter how hard he works he is passed over for advancement by others who are less deserving. Eventually, he's pushed out and has to find a new job where the same scenario unfolds. I've suggested, without much success, that the way to be free of this personal pattern is to explore it. The difficulty is that the source of this pattern is buried in the subconscious and guarded by insecurities. I hope that one day, with enough support and compassion, my friend will be willing to look within and find it.

## Remembering the Loss

For many, perhaps most, professionals in the corporate world the path forward is not always one natural step up after another. People experience setbacks, learn from them or not, and move on. If the setbacks keep coming it can be deeply discouraging. In these cases, is there something contributing to the pattern of not getting ahead that is below the threshold of awareness? Is something unresolved that needs to be seen and addressed?

Ann wondered why in her job search she kept being ranked as the second or third most desirable candidate. Not getting the job was bad enough, but what made it so disappointing was that she had been brought back for numerous follow-up interviews to no avail. She was a strong candidate with good credentials and references. What kept getting in her way of landing the job she wanted and was qualified for? The feedback from the hiring organization was always positive, yet the offer still went to someone else. In the constellation we had, she set up one representative for the typical hiring organization and one for herself. The representatives took about a minute to tune into what they noticed. The hiring *organization* was looking up with a faraway gaze. Ann was looking in the direction of the *organization.*

I stood next to the wall that the *organization* was looking at and then placed a person there to represent the unknown element he was gazing at. Who or what did this person represent? The eye contact between the unknown representative and the *organization* had the feeling of an unresolved family issue. I asked Ann if it was okay if I posed a personal question. She affirmed it was. She knew she could choose to answer it or not. I asked if her mother had lost a child or a lover. Ann replied that her mother had had an abortion between her own birth and that of her older brother. Although there was no judgment in the room about the abortion, it was something that seemed to be related to Ann's current situation. "Do you want to continue to explore this very sensitive and personal issue?" I asked. Ann was firm that she did want to continue. A representative was brought in for Ann's brother. Ann said that after her mother had told her about the abortion she had thought often about the sibling—perhaps a sister—she missed having. The representative for this sibling (Sib) was asked to sit on the floor and face her *mother.*

The *mother* told the *sibling* she always had a place in her heart for her as her child. Once the bond between them was acknowledged they faced the two living siblings, *Ann* and *her brother (Bro)*. Their *mother* told them that she took full responsibility for what she had done. They were blameless. They were free to live their own lives and do something good with them.

Ann acknowledged her unborn *sibling* as the older child who came before her. *She* honored her *sibling's* and her *mother's* fates and asked them to look kindly on her as she led her own life. *She* would do something good with her life in memory of her *sibling* without feeling that she had to atone for what happened.

**Reflections:** Is it fair to question any link between an abortion and a job search? The fair answer is nothing and maybe everything, depending on how the circumstances unfolded. Things happen, and sometimes people, especially children, take responsibility for these occurrences even though they were innocent bystanders. Ann may have unconsciously decided she had to atone for the loss of her unborn sibling. She may have believed that it was the nature of life to withhold part of itself from her. While this is conjecture, we do know that a problem can arise when two seemingly unrelated issues are unconsciously linked. If the constellation surfaces that link, and the issue holder wants to explore it, then I believe it's best to trust the insights that are uncovered. Choosing not to know is not necessarily the safest or most pain-free option.

Two aspects of this constellation are important for the new facilitator to remember. The first is to ask the issue holder if she wants to proceed when sensitive personal information starts to surface. As you gain experience, you will sense when the issue behind the issue is something the issue holder might want to keep private. The second is to protect the issue holder from disruptive questions or comments. Other participants may not realize just how emotionally vulnerable the issue holder might be feeling.

Analytical questions and comments interrupt the inner, healing movements. After dealing with a sensitive issue like Ann did, the issue holder may need a few minutes alone to collect herself. The group can debrief while the person is out of the room and out of earshot.

## More Searching for Success

Ted, a slender man in his thirties, wanted clarity about his next career move. He was considering a number of possibilities and was uncertain about where he should focus. His interests seemed so broad and varied that I was moved to say, "You can't be God and have all possibilities. At some point you need to say Yes to one thing and No to others." Ted agreed, and he revealed that he was running out of unemployment benefits in a couple of months. Soon he would either return to working in a service industry or find a way to be self-employed. Upon further questioning it came out that he had not really felt successful in any aspect of his life: career, relationships, finances, and even health. The fundamental question was, what was blocking his success? He had no idea why his life had turned out the way it had. Ironically, his siblings were exceptionally successful in their careers.

Ted picked representatives for himself, success, and the obstacle to it, and then set them up. Almost immediately the *obstacle* walked up to *Ted* and, standing by his side, took his arm in a loving way. *Ted* looked unhappy with this sudden show of affection or solidarity. *Success* began looking intently at a doorway on the other side of the room and paid no attention to the others. The actual Ted was at a loss as to why the block to success seemed so aligned with him. He mentioned as he scratched himself that he had had a medical condition for many years that burned and itched.

I selected a representative for the condition and placed her in the constellation.

*She* reported being uncomfortable, but there seemed to be no significant change with the other representatives after she found her place.

Somewhere in Ted's family, I thought, there must be a triggering event connected to the rest of the constellated system. It was a small group, and we were running out of participants to call upon. I wrote on a piece of paper the word "source" and found a place in the room where that part of the system seemed to belong. Almost immediately, I dropped down, as if I had been knocked down to the ground.

*"Who was killed?"* I asked lying prone on the floor. *"Who was blown up? Was there a fire?"* Ted reported that when his mother was a young woman her boyfriend had been killed in a plane crash. The addition of the *dead lover* brought *success* to her knees. She could not look in his direction and covered her eyes. The *medical condition* was taken out of that role and placed next to the dead lover as a representative for Ted's mother. The *mother* reported that she felt cold and distant. The real Ted stood beside her and said to his *mother, "I grieved for you."*

Other phrases were given to Ted to help break his unconscious identification with the *dead lover* and his mother's grief. Responding to his words Ted's *mother* acknowledged him. She would grieve her loss. He was her son and he had his own life to live and enjoy. Inspired by his *mother's* blessing Ted promptly strode over to *success* and brought her to her feet so she could stand beside him. The *obstacle* now was sitting down and turned away. *Success* felt pressured. Ted was trying too hard to take hold of her. He needed to slow down and allow her to engage with him at her own pace. Seeing how Ted was overreaching

I took myself out of the role of the *dead lover* and brought the constellation to an end.

**Reflections:** Ted's challenges with success and his health condition appeared to be linked to his identification with his mother's boyfriend, who died in a plane crash. We didn't know for certain, but Ted's persistent medical condition suggested the boyfriend's death was related to a fire that was part of the crash. Even in death, the boyfriend was still part of Ted's family system. By acknowledging his place, his mother's loss, and how those circumstances affected his family, Ted could start to free himself from an entanglement in a tragedy that occurred before he was born.

## More Ted

Ted returned for another constellation about a year after the first one. This time he spoke more directly about what he wanted but was not getting out life. Although his medical condition was better, he still felt like a failure. Every job he held ended or led to a dead end. His relationships with women never seemed to go anywhere. He had tried years earlier to join a religious order, but that did not work out either. He set goals but always found ways to distract himself from achieving them. The only comfort he had was his addiction to food and the Internet.

A constellation was set up with his life goals, his addictions *(Addict),* and himself. Almost immediately Ted's representative looked at a place on the floor behind *addictions* and in front of *goals. Ted* reported feeling sad. A representative for someone or something *deceased* was placed there. The representative felt she was Ted's dreams and aspirations that never happened. Adding to Ted's angst was the fact that his siblings and father were all successful and accomplished. In comparison, he felt his life was nothing and he had nothing. He could not relate to his own family.

"Was everyone in this family successful except you?" I asked. Ted remembered that one of his grandfathers had gone through a bankruptcy and a very public failure. A representative for his grandfather was placed in the constellation. *Ted* and his *grandfather* felt sympathy for each other, but not a strong connection. A representative was placed near the grandfather as the source of Ted's angst. Ted, who had taken his place in the constellation, advanced as if to confront an adversary. The source felt that he wasn't a personality or spirit that could be related to as a friend or foe. He was more like some law of nature that just was. *Addictions* wanted to circle Ted and protect him by plugging the holes between Ted and the *source*. Ted literally sank down into a place of hopelessness. I asked Ted to look at his life and acknowledge its emptiness and aloneness, and to agree to it. It was the way it was even if why was a mystery. *A good solution* was placed nearby overlooking Ted and his life. Both *addictions* and the *source* moved back several steps when the *good solution* was introduced.

Ted looked at the *good solution* and began to express his doubts that it was real. He had seen solutions that promised him much yet led to nothing. He could not believe this was any different. When they heard this, *addictions* and the *source* moved back toward Ted where they had been before. In response, I introduced *Faith* as part of the good solution. Ted backed away, saying he did not trust them. I took his move to indicate that Ted did not trust life. What was the root cause of this distrust? I questioned Ted about his childhood. "Had he been a premature baby?" No, but when he was six months old he had been hospitalized with a severe illness and was separated from his mother. He had almost died, but he revived when she came to see him.

I asked representatives for *life* to go to *baby Ted's* side and hold him. *"I will never leave you. I will always be with you,"* one of them told him. *Baby Ted* beamed. The adult Ted took them both into his arms. The room felt like it was filling up with a warm glow. Ted looked at his *goals* and his successful family. *Life* transformed into a woman. Ted introduced her to his family as his partner. Embracing *life* he reached out to embrace living it fully.

**Reflections:** Trauma, especially trauma that is forgotten or unacknowledged, can leave a deep, yet hidden imprint on the psyche. The bond with the mother is the source of life. If that bond is disrupted, can the child ever trust or have faith in life? When life is not trusted, it is more difficult to give and receive. The deprived child becomes a needy adult who does not know why he is needy or how to meet those needs. A rupture in the parent-child relationship and a lack of bonding between them have been shown to have an impact on the development of the child's prefrontal cortex according to researchers like Daniel Siegel.[2]

About a year later I saw Ted and asked him how everything was going. Ted smiled and replied that he felt his life had turned around. His health was good and his addictions had less of a grip. He had found work that he liked, and he was doing better with relationships. I was happy for Ted and glad to hear his good news. Life is complex, and many factors, known and unknown, contribute to an outcome. As long as Ted felt, as he did, that systemic work supported the shifts he wanted, that acknowledgment was enough.

**More Reflections:** Most psychologists would agree that a loving relationship with your mother as a child benefits your life as an adult. Family therapist Bert Hellinger, observing the legacy of this relationship in many of his clients, wrote, *"The early interruption of the movement to the mother (by the child) has far-reaching consequences for our life and our success later on."*[3]

One of the findings of a study that followed 268 Harvard undergraduate men for 75 years spelled out those benefits in financial terms. The study was conducted by the Harvard Medical School and was part of a larger program focused on the study of adult development. The men in the study "who had 'warm' childhood relationships with their mothers earned an average of 87,000 dollars more a year than  men whose relationships were uncaring."[4] The study also  found that "men's boyhood relationships with their mothers—but not their fathers—were associated with effectiveness at work."[5]

## All in the Family

A group of siblings owned and operated a chain of stores, all of which were doing well except one; it was the perennial problem child that seriously underperformed. This puzzled the siblings because the store had everything going for it, like its great location, that generally predicted success. For some reason, though, the store's clerks and managers never jelled as a team and turnover was high. The siblings had a track record of success so why was this store the holdout? They were considering selling it and cutting their losses.

One of the siblings decided to try a constellation before agreeing to the sale. During our discussion, I wondered if something had happened at the location in the past that was somehow influencing those who currently worked there. We set up two representatives: one for the location and the other for the owners. The representative for the owners seemed puzzled and disconnected. The representative for the location was sick to his stomach and felt a sense of alienation. He stepped back as far as he could. A representative was added for the source of his alienation. He sank to the ground looking depressed and isolated.

When questioned about the family's history, the sibling recalled that the store had originally been owned by another family member. She asked the siblings to take it over and run it because it was losing money. I wondered if her loss would have been the siblings' gain if they had turned the store around. If they looked good the family member might look bad and resent their success. Perhaps out of loyalty the siblings wanted to avoid creating a division in the family. When the representative for the location heard this, he felt better, but he still kept his distance. What else might have happened?

Another family member had been working at the store as the manager before the siblings took it over. His representative stood in front of the source of the alienation as if to hide it. He appeared cocky, seemingly sure he was getting away with something. The representative for the sibling looked at him and the location and was asked to say, "We will find out what happened here and put things right." At first the manager seemed defiant. He moved away from the source and stood by a person who represented the original owner. When she ignored him, he moved to a wall and faced it, as though he was ashamed of himself. The location looked happier when he heard the sibling voice his resolve. He moved closer, ready to engage. He felt like he represented the staff of the store as well as the location. The sibling was asked to tell the manager, "We will hold you accountable, but we won't exclude or humiliate you. You are still part of our family." The manager turned back around, looking sheepish and a bit chastised.

**Reflections:** Whatever had occurred during the tenure of

the manager needed to be brought to light. It was a family secret that created pressure in the system as long as it was suppressed. Family-based loyalty to the original owner and manager may have blinded the siblings to issues that should have been addressed and resolved before they took the store over. The staff for the store appeared to feel the unresolved energy of the secret and act it out. The sibling who asked for the constellation left with a number of challenges. Could she convince her siblings there was a family secret that needed to be revealed? And, if so, could she uncover and deal with what had happened during the tenure of the original manager? Selling the store might not resolve the issue if the secret still affected their business dealings as a family.

## Chapter 17
# Just in Time Constellating

The case studies in this chapter are difficult to categorize. Since they have aspects of both management and professional constellations I am putting them in their own category. They illustrate "just in time constellating" because they are about working systemically in the urgency of the moment. When the wheels of your program are about to wobble off, how do you respond systemically?

### Type-A Paralysis

A leadership team I was working with was composed of smart, articulate type-A executives. They led an international organization that had staff in thirty countries. The backgrounds of the executives were as diverse as the countries they operated in. Because they were spread over four continents, they came together annually for a weeklong planning retreat to redefine business areas, set targets, and align resources. They faced a great deal of complexity and ambiguity in their current environment, but there was no point in waiting for things to sort themselves out. If they did not decide on their strategic objectives events would soon decide for them.

One shared concern was the challenge of making a decision as a group. They all held strong views and the tendency to speak at length about them. Could the team make a decision they were clear about and committed to implementing? As outspoken leaders, they knew they were difficult to lead as a group. At previous leadership meetings, for instance, they had exhausted themselves in lengthy debates. When time ran out they ended up with ambiguous agreements that sidestepped the more divisive issues. Naturally, they looked to their boss to break the verbal logjams and make the final decisions. He was adamant, in response, that he would not be the sole decider. The team had to reach a working consensus. Otherwise, once the executives returned to their respective countries, the buy-in needed to ensure implementation would be lacking. During the initial two days of the retreat, the extensive planning and detailed preparations for the meeting enabled the leaders to make good progress. The first two discussion areas were vigorously debated yet still resulted in decisions supported by everyone.

On the third day, however, people started to tire. Reasoned debate took on the tone of bickering and irritation. How things were being said was getting in the way of how others were hearing it. Different points of view over minor concerns suddenly became irreconcilable differences. The complexity and interrelatedness of the issues were more logs piling on the rapidly growing jam. I called for a break. Most of the participants left the room to get coffee and walk off their frustrations. Others opened up their laptops to answer emails. In the back of the room, unnoticed, I took a few minutes to set up the dynamic that was unfolding. There was the management team, the analysis paralysis that was occurring, and its source. As a visual aid for myself, I drew the diagram shown in Figure 17-1.

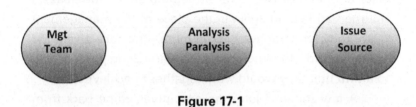

**Figure 17-1**

In my mind's eye I transposed the diagram to the floor and then I went and stood in each spot as I walked through the system I was dealing with. I started with the *management team.* They felt weak and fragmented, literally spinning in small circles. The *analysis paralysis* felt strong and arrogant. I could almost hear it boast to the other parts, *"I am in charge here. I am on top."* The *source* of the analysis paralysis also felt weak and distant, as though it was in the past. I introduced the *purpose* of the organization as the fourth part of the current dynamic. Its place also seemed to be off at a distance; it was not really noticed by the others and was waiting for something to be resolved.

I focused my attention on the people and forces who were the source behind the analysis paralysis. I could not tell if they had been victims or perpetrators, or perhaps both. Something like an act of nature mixed up with cultural belief systems came to mind. The term *"race consciousness"* defines the mix of archaic beliefs and experiences underlying the long history of human conflict. Since the executives came from different countries on different continents, their lives were likely shaped by the forces and events that pitted different nationalities, races, religions, and ethnic groups against each other. I marked a place on the floor to represent the peoples and groups that had been, or were now, caught up in those collective conflicts and traumas. I stood a few feet away on a place of universal healing light and love and asked that light to be present for them. After a minute or two, I felt something shift and release. I returned and stood again in the place of the management team. They felt stronger. I asked them—the collective mind of their group—to remember their overarching purpose and to affirm that they would work together to achieve it.

A few minutes later the executives came back from their break and resumed their discussions. The previous points of dissension were forgotten and they addressed the substantive issues without the same level of rancor. When they came to another controversial issue, someone asked a question that shifted the potential dispute into a collaborative exercise filled with friendly laughter. While the executives still needed skilled facilitation and a variety of interventions to keep them on track, at the end of each day they expressed their delight and surprise over the progress they made. At one point their leader gave me a puzzled look and in a low voice said, *"I can't believe how well behaved everyone is."* I gave him a knowing look and nodded my head.

## Things Are Not Always as They Seem

A new unit grew in a few years into a large organization that reported to one manager. This growth in the scope of activities and the number of staff required a change in its structure. The unit was reorganized into teams and team leaders were promoted from the original group. Although more than two years had lapsed since the reorganization, this was still a contentious issue for those who had not been selected and felt hurt by the loss of status. The manager and his team leaders embarked on a lengthy process of engaging staff to find ways to address their concerns and refocus attention on the larger purpose of the unit. The scope of their efforts included surveys, off-site retreats, training, working groups, and various initiatives to implement the resulting recommendations. Despite these initiatives there was still a resentful group whose negativity was a drag on others.

According to change theory, this is to be expected. A small percentage of staff will always support a major change initiative while an equally small percentage will oppose it. The group to focus on is the large one in the middle of the bell curve; they will respond to a sensible plan that lays out why the change is needed and how it will be accomplished. Because of HR constraints firing the persistently negative staff was not an option. What else could be done to mitigate their impact?

After spending the day with the leadership team, I spent the evening conducting an introductory session on organizational constellations for a professional association. It rarely happens, yet at this meeting no one volunteered a business challenge to constellate. Since the issue was on my mind, I set up the dynamic I had been discussing with the leadership team earlier in the day. My goal was to gain insight, as a team coach, on how the unit leader and his team leaders could resolve this sticky problem.

I chose four representatives: the management team, staff who were engaged and had a positive outlook, those who a negative outlook, and the source of the issue that had plagued the unit. The representatives found their places and arranged themselves without much adjustment. Soon the *source* of the issue sank to the floor. She gazed at *management (Mgt)* and after a while crawled a few feet to be next to him. The *negative staff (Neg)* also looked at management. *Positive staff (Pos)* stared at the *source. Management* tried to look back at the *source* but could not bring himself to turn toward it. I brought in another person to represent his resistance *(Resist)* to looking. *Management* was then able to turn and acknowledge *source* and the impact it had on her. *Resistance* at first felt an urge to get away from the *source.* She relaxed once *management* engaged with it. During this exchange, the *positive staff* carefully edged away from *negative staff* till he found a spot where *management* stood between them. *Negative staff* moved closer to *management.* (The positions of the representatives at this point in the constellation are shown in Figure 17-2.)

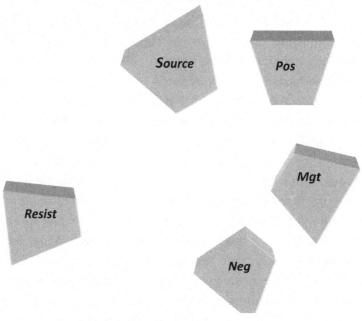

**Figure 17-2**

The *positive staff* glanced fearfully at the *negative staff. Negative staff* felt drawn to *management* with the intention of being helpful. *Management,* which had become the individual manager of the unit and not the management team, felt a connection to the source. The source did not know if she was a person or an event. *Negative staff* expressed her desire to support the *manager* in dealing with the *source*. *Source* stood up and looked expectantly toward the *manager*. I asked the *source* and the *manager* if the intensity of how they interacted with each other was related to something in the manager's own system. They both felt that was the case. The *manager* affirmed that the source was her issue to see and deal with. It was part of who she was and had a place in her life. The staff began to relax. *Positive staff* felt better, but he still had some fear or uneasiness about *negative staff* and looked to the *manager* for protection. The *manager* assured positive staff that he would maintain a safe and respectful workplace. *Positive staff* relaxed somewhat but still seemed concerned. The *manager,* the *source*, and *negative staff* stood facing each other in a friendly manner and then embraced as *positive staff* and *resistance* looked on.

**Reflections:** The constellation produced insights I would not have gained by other means. The challenge now was to find ways to apply those insights. I considered two possible next steps. One was to communicate to the management team that they should be more proactive in protecting others from the behaviors of the negative staff. People who are habitually resentful toward their managers can also be just as quick to find reasons to resent their coworkers. More action to explain the norms and hold people accountable to them seemed needed. The other step was a private coaching session with the manager. I found it intriguing that negative staff were actually in some unconscious way in service to him. Their behaviors might be giving voice to part of the manager's own personal history that needed expression. Perhaps the dysfunctions of the small group were a call for deeper introspection into his own use of self.

Because of his own personal history, was the manager somehow giving the negative group a free pass? Avoiding conflict will not foster a healthy work environment.

A few months later I returned to conduct another training session with the same management team. Surprisingly, things had settled down with the difficult team members, especially with one person who had been consistently disruptive. The leader had not taken any overt action, like a counseling session, that could explain the shift. And he was reluctant to initiate any action now that might disrupt the new status quo. I asked when the shift occurred and was told it had been around the time of their last training session. While this was good news, there was no way of knowing if the constellation that evening after the training had an impact on staff behavior. It did become clear over time that the manager needed to be firmer and more assertive in defining and upholding the standards of behavior expected in the workplace.

## Addressing the BOQs

The constellation methodology has the potential to enhance how an organization and its leaders function. So far, only a miniscule fraction of that potential has been realized in the corporate world. Eventually, awareness of this tool will become more widespread and it will be used to address big organizational questions (BOQs). Although careful analytics are helpful, there are some problems and issues where something more is needed to find the solution.

The typical BOQ has strategic and far-reaching consequences. The firm may be "betting the farm," so to speak, on the decision. Getting it right will be good for the organization. Getting it wrong could prove costly, even fatal. Think of a major merger, succession planning, defusing interpersonal conflict, developing a new strategy, restructuring, managing brands, maintaining competitiveness, or resolving some persistent issue that has been unresponsive to other interventions. The public sector grapples with many of the same questions around strategy and restructuring. Because the decision-making powers are usually more diffused, organizational change is like enduring a year-long root canal. The constellation process provides unique insights into public sector BOQs as well as social and environmental change efforts. Recall, for example, that the whole of chapter 14 ("Reconciling the Irreconcilable") explores the Israeli-Palestinian conflict and America's role in facilitating the peace talks between the two groups.

In the private sector the challenge of completing a successful merger is an example of a decision-making process that needs shoring up. According to the investment firm T. Rowe Price, the success rate for mergers may be less than 50 percent. The reasons why *"Few companies can really do it well"* include the lack of management capacity and differences in culture between the merging firms.[1] Managerial analytics might seem to justify the merger; however, the human factors will determine whether or not two diverse groups are able to merge into one synergetic whole. Various well-known and successful executives, like Konrad Hilton, have shared how they trust their gut when faced with a critical decision. Similarly, the constellation process gives the executive team a methodology for applying their intuition in a structured and visible manner. An open enrollment constellation workshop may be too public of a forum; what other ways, therefore, can a management team use to access this tool?

### Rent-a-Rep for a BOQ

There two ways an executive team can bring the constellation process to bear on a BOQ. One is to bring in an organizational development consultant whose skill set includes the constellation methodology. The advantage of this approach is that you have someone who brings a depth of contextual knowledge and a variety of methods for facilitating change in addition to constellations. The other way is to contract with a facilitator with a mandate limited to setting up and conducting the constellation. While skilled in constellation work, however, the facilitator may be less knowledgeable about the context of working in an organization.

The facilitator may propose asking other people from outside the organization to serve as representatives. Using one or more "rent-a-reps" ensures that the constellation will be conducted with representatives who will not skew the outcome because of their insider knowledge or preexisting relationships. Allowing and reporting in a neutral manner on what is noticed physically, emotionally, and mentally are all traits of an experienced representative. In a long-term engagement, the executive team could develop their own representational skills. In the short term, the rent-a-rep offers a convenient way to introduce the process. In most high-stakes BOQs, the additional cost of a constellation will not be a consideration, given what is at stake.

Senior executives with major organizations in Europe and North America have used both of the above approaches. The issues are sensitive, so the representatives and facilitator agree to maintain confidentially. What happens there stays there, along with the identity of the clients.

# PART III

# Obtaining Your
# Learner's Permit

*The case studies in the previous chapters show how con-stellations have been used to bring about insight and change in the workplace. The next step is to develop your own capacity to work systemically with your clients or team. A number of structured exercises are provided since they offer the new systemic leader an accessible point of entry for mastering this practice. Eventually, constellations will become a well-known and accepted methodology that addresses a wide diversity of urgent challenges in the workplace.*

## Chapter 18
# How Do You Learn to Do This?

**A**reoccurring comment and question I get from others when they see this work is, *"This is pretty cool. How do I learn to do it?"* The answer, of course, is it depends. You can start incorporating the concepts in this book into your own consulting practice or leadership activities right away. Review the case studies and look for similar situations when you could apply the insights they offer. In mastering any new skill, training is essential. Basic and advanced yearlong train-the-facilitator programs are available in Europe and North and South America. The programs typically consist of four or five workshops, each lasting three or four days, conducted over the time frame of a year.

Training is important, but mastery comes through practice: the more the better. Participating in a practice group develops the confidence and experience needed to work with the public. Other facilitators and I have observed that when you begin to facilitate systemically you get the level of difficulty you are ready to handle. Those with more skill and experience tend to end up facilitating clients with more complex, traumatic, and charged issues.

The principles related to organizational constellations are similar to those followed in family constellations. Even though most training programs focus on family or personal issues, the skill set gained can be used by the business-orientated facilitator. In both cases the facilitator helps the client define the issue and then look for the underlying systemic cause that is driving it. The business facilitator does need to keep in mind that an organization differs greatly from a family. These differences, like the right to belong, will inform how the constellation is set up, conducted, and discussed afterward. As mentioned before, facilitated sessions can and will go awry when these differences are not taken into account. The upshot is that organizational facilitators or leaders will benefit from reading and applying the material in this book.

Learning and practicing the principles behind organizational constellations is one form of preparation. If you are drawn to this methodology most likely you already engage in some form of self-development through meditation, therapy, yoga, or journaling, just to name a few. The path you follow is less important than the fact that you are on one. I've been at this since I was sixteen years old and came across a copy of Aldous Huxley's classic *The Perennial Philosophy.*[1] Even after forty-plus years of meditation and many different methods for personal development, I am still open to new ways to grow. At some point in your development, the old adage *"When the student is ready the teacher appears"* shifts and becomes, for you, *"When the teacher is ready the student appears."*

While most of the action in systemic constellation work is in Europe, many workshops and conferences are offered in other parts of the world. The website http://www. talent-manager.pt, maintained by the organizational constellation facilitator Cecillo Regojo, offers a current listing of international workshops, conferences, and training programs related to family and organizational constellations. For the workshops I offer, please check my website, http:// teambuildingassociates.com.

It is useful to remember that different proponents of this method will have their own take on how the methodology should be set up and practiced. As more books are published, what you read in this one will differ compared to what others write or teach. The methodology is evolving as our understanding of individual and group behavior deepens. There is no officially approved school of organizational constellations that decides how things should be done. Individual facilitators like myself offer our own train-the-trainer workshops. In time, like the field of executive coaching, a point may be reached where the practice is widespread enough to support a certifying association.

The corporate shaman approach of working with the subconscious augments but does not replace the standard methodologies used for group facilitation, consulting, or leadership. Tools and methods such as Action Learning,[2] the Emotional Quotient Inventory (EQi),[3] and Situational Leadership[4] will continue to be a vital part of leadership and organizational development initiatives.

### Explaining the Unexplainable

How do you explain a nonlinear and non-conceptual concept? Explanations are inherently linear and conceptual. A new concept that is not yet part of the societal norm adds to the challenge. People who are literal and detail-oriented and task and time focused make excellent administrators. You can rely on them to pay attention to details and deadlines. It is also likely that their patience or appreciation for anything metaphysical in theory and subjective in practice is limited. While constellations are the ultimate hands-on problem-solving tool, they are also outside the usual frame of reference that constitutes the established worldview. The quickest way to dig a hole that is steep and deep with a literal-minded client is to spend a lot of time explaining the process. Rational explanations don't explain a nonrational process. One option is to just do a constellation after a brief introduction. If the potential issue holder is eager to find a solution, as opposed to complain about a problem, it's a good sign he is ready. People who have a sense of urgency are not so concerned with theories and supportive evidence. They just want help with their problem and are ready to do the work that is required.

The exercises and activities offered in the next chapter are the best explanations you can give to a group new to this work, especially if people are a bit skeptical. Personal experience is a much better instructor and far more convincing than any expert can be. Encouraging people to see for themselves builds trust and cooperation.

## Chapter 19

# Exploring the Field with Structured Exercises

This chapter offers seven constellation exercises you can do by yourself or with others to deepen your understanding of the process and the benefits it offers.

### 1. Accessing the Field

This exercise was presented in chapter 4 ("Third Pillar: The Knowing Field") as a way to introduce yourself and others to the practice of accessing the field. It is summarized here for your convenience in the following steps:

    **a.** Three people gather to form a triad. One person will be the experimenter and the other two will be the subjects. The experimenter thinks of someone whom they have an intense relationship with. The relationship could be positive or negative but not so negative that he fears for his safety.

    **b.** The experimenter selects one of the subjects to represent himself and the other subject to

represent the person who is the intense relationship. Without telling the subjects whom they
represent, position them a few feet apart.

c. The experimenter then touches each subject on
the shoulder with the quiet intention in mind of
who that subject represents. The subjects are
given a minute or two to just notice what they
notice, without any agenda. If they feel the inspiration to move or turn in some direction they
should slowly follow their inner prompting.

d. The subjects report out what they feel somatically about themselves and the other person.
Generally, the experimenter will find that the
subjects are surprisingly accurate. The source of
their knowledge is hidden from view. Yet, they
are still able to access that knowledge even if
they don't know how or where they obtained it.

## 2. The Challenge

Here is a tool to focus your creative potential on addressing a business or personal challenge. You can do this
for yourself or you can coach another person through this
process by following the steps listed below:

a. Take several 3-by-5 cards and a pen. Breathe
deeply and center yourself. Think about and
define your challenge or question.

b. Write on one card a brief description of your
challenge or question. Ten words or fewer are
best. This is an important step because a clear
idea of your challenge or question is needed in
order to get a clear answer.

c. Place that card on the floor or a desktop. Write
another card with just your name on it and place

that where it seems most appropriate in rela-
tion to the first card. Notice what comes to mind
when you look at the two cards and how they are
placed in relationship to each other. Notice any
images or feelings that arise.

**d.** What other factors have a significant impact on
you and your challenge? Write each one down on
a card in a few words. Place them where you feel
they belong in relationship to the other cards. A
factor can be a relevant person, an idea/concept,
a thing, a department or team, or a resource that
is a part of the challenge. For simplicity's sake,
focus on six or less of the most significant factors.

**e.** Notice if anything changes in your thoughts or
feelings when you place a card down. The cards
should be placed far enough apart so you can
move around and stand on or behind each one and
see the other cards from that particular perspective. How does one of the factors on a card see
your challenge from its perspective? How does it
see the other factors that impact the challenge?
What does it need to say to those other factors?

**f.** Return to your own card. Now that you have
seen the challenge from other perspectives and
given voice to the concerns or requests of those
perspectives, has anything changed for you?
Has your own perspective shifted in some way?
Did you have to suspend a judgment or assump-
tion? Is there more space for a creative solution
or insight to emerge?

**g.** Take a card and write down any new ideas,
insights, or solutions that come to mind. Evaluate
your list for an idea you can act on.

### 3. Inner Strengths Finder Exercise

When facing a challenge, what gives you strength and confidence? Are you able to call on those inner resources when you feel you are on your own? The way I worked with Jan in the case study "Gaining Confidence" (see chapter 15, "Professional Constellations") is an example of how the inner strengths exercise is facilitated for an issue holder.

> **a.** Create a list of the different sources of strength and confidence you can draw upon. These sources typically include such aspects of your life as Education, Training, Family, Ancestors, Friends, Previous Successes, Mentors and Supporters, Personal Values, Philosophy, Nature, a Sacred Place, Religion, your Higher Power, and Spiritual Deity or Saint.
>
> **b.** Think of the way you would like to represent these sources of strength and wisdom. You can write them down on a card or use pictures or photos. If you are in a group setting, you can ask people to represent the sources.
>
> **c.** Line up the cards or persons. Move from one to the other. Take time to take in the blessing each representative offers you. If you feel inspired to express some words of gratitude, go ahead. If the representative has something encouraging to say, listen with an open heart.
>
> **d.** After connecting consciously with your sources of strength and wisdom, turn and face your challenge. How do you feel now compared to how you felt before this exercise?

This exercise, setting up representatives for the issue holder's resources and his challenges, worked well for a professional who was going on a mission to a politically unstable part of Africa. He knew the complex environment would figuratively and literally contain landmine-like issues that could explode with unpleasant consequences with one misstep. His resources came together to support him and strengthen his ability to anticipate and respond effectively in that unstable environment.

## 4. Work-Life Balance

Like the weather, there is a great deal of talk in the workplace about work-life balance, but little is done to change it. The following activity can lead to insights that are life changing:

a. Join up with two other people. Ask one to represent your personal life and the other to represent your work life.

b. Position them in relationship to yourself and then wait and notice what you notice. If anyone feels an impulse to move do so slowly.

c. Notice the direction the representatives are facing and how your relationship with them feels. Do you sense a better or more harmonious relationship with one rather than the other? How much does this mirror your actual life? What do you need to say to foster a healthy, happy relationship with both parts of your life? What feedback or advice do the two representatives have for you?

d. Take a few minutes to debrief the exercise and then switch roles.

### 5. Money & You

Money and self-love influence each other in the same way that work life and home life affect each other. Explore this dynamic by doing the following:

**a.** Choose a representative for money.

**b.** Set up *money* and *you.*

**c.** Notice how *money* relates to *you* and *you* relate to *money.* Notice if there is some distance or alienation between you.

**d.** If so, test out a few phrases to see if closeness or harmony can be restored. For example, tell money, *"You have a place in my life"* or *"We do good things together."*

**e.** Notice if *money* morphs into something or someone else. When you look at money, do you also see someone who is nurturing? If not, do you see someone or something that is not nurturing or life supportive?

**f.** Discuss what you noticed with your partner. Depending on what showed up, you might be getting a call for a deeper exploration of your core beliefs and the connection between money and love in your life.

### 6. Chaos Constellation

Sometimes a problem, like the proverbial peace of God, passes all understanding. Letting go of the need to understand makes it possible to draw upon the perspective of the subconscious. The issue holder can still provide background his challenge, however; a lot of detail is not required or desired for this exercise.

**a.** The issue holder stands in the center of the room representing him- or herself.

**b.** Each participant in the room steps into the knowing field in the timing and manner they feel guided to take. It does not matter; there are no assignments. Holding the intention to represent an aspect of the problem or challenge is enough.

**c.** The representatives follow their inner movements and speak or move as they feel inspired.

**d.** The facilitator starts and observes the interactions and ends the constellation when it appears complete.

**e.** The issue holder notices if anything feels different concerning his or her issue and if he or she has any new inspirations or realizations.

## 7. Problem Constellation

A goal is the results someone wants to achieve in the world. If it does not happen then that person has a problem. According to therapist Virginia Satir, *"The problem is never the problem; it is only a symptom of something much deeper."*[1] If the issue holder really knew what the problem was about, he or she would have taken the steps needed to solve it. The problem constellation offers a template that helps uncover what stands behind the symptom. The symptom is visible, but its source and purpose are hidden in the shadows of the subconscious. The professional constellation I facilitated for Lee, the business coach you read about in the "Hidden Obstacle" case study in chapter 15, follows this template.

**a.** The parts of the template for the problem constellation include: the issue holder, the goal/objective, the obstacle (the problem/issue that is blocking progress), and the payoff—which may or may not be hidden.

**b.** It is best to start with just these few parts. If needed, you can add other parts, such as: stakeholders, activities to achieve the goal, staff who carry out those activities, clients/customers, and the vision or larger purpose of what the issue holder is trying to achieve.

**c.** Have the issue holder set up the representatives in relationship to each other.

**d.** Pay attention to the payoff. What is the relationship between the payoff and the obstacle? Is the payoff hidden? What does the stakeholder need to say to the payoff that mitigates the obstacle? Are there any internal or external resources that the stakeholder should be drawing upon? Allow those interactions to unfold without trying to achieve a predetermined outcome.

**e.** Debrief with the issue holder what he observed and the insights he obtained. What did he learn about the obstacle and the payoff and their relationship to his goal? How will he apply that learning?

## A Coaching Tool One-on-One

While the preceding constellations exercises rely on representatives, an executive coach with just the client in the room could use 3-by-5 cards to represent the different parts of the client's issue. After placing the cards on the floor, the coach or the client should simply move from one card to another and share the perspective of that part of the system, be it a person, an idea, or a thing written on a card. Insight is gained by looking within in a nonverbal manner and noticing feelings, thoughts, and sensations.

This bypasses the tendency of the verbal and rational mind to explain, deny, and defend. The facilitator supplies healing phrases that, when expressed by the client, inwardly restore harmony and resolve contradictions. As the client gains more self-awareness, limitations related to his or her frozen past are surfaced and resolved.

## Chapter 20
# Summary Thoughts

Having read this far you are well aware that the challenges the issue holders in the case studies faced are also opportunities. A case study or two may even have dealt with an issue or a trauma you also are struggling with. The good news is that the shift experienced by the issue holder is, to some extent, available to you, the reader. Understandably, it is hard to see any gift in your challenge, issue, or obstacle, especially if it brings up significant emotional distress. Finding that gift is more likely when you stop resisting reality and stay fully present for at least a few minutes with "what is."

This approach is self-affirming. Your workplace dramas are reenactments of the parts of your life that are denied, excluded, or unresolved. The dramas reoccur and you stay stuck in unproductive reactions as long as you continue to hide those parts from yourself. See them without judgment. Embrace them, and they will reintegrate. When you welcome those lost parts home, new competencies for self-leadership and the leadership of others will emerge.

According to Steve Jobs, a disruptive innovation is not likely to come out of a focus group. Jobs quoted Henry Ford as saying that if he had asked customers what they wanted they would have told him a faster horse.[1] Visionary leaders like Jobs and Ford are willing to try something radically different that no one else is doing. There will always be those who defend the status quo through disbelief and ridicule of an innovative idea whose outcome is uncertain and the process risky. Until, that is, everyone agrees it was obviously a good idea all along.

Back in 1991, when ropes courses were still a new and somewhat controversial phenomena for corporate groups, I wrote a book called *The Power of Team-Building Using Ropes Techniques*.[2] Learning through hands-on, interactive activities was dismissed by critics as frivolous fun and silly games. Gradually, people realized that listening to lectures all day did little to actually teach the skills of teamwork and leadership. Whether you go outside today or not, the action learning principles that we used as ropes course facilitators are now embedded in the leadership training industry.

Something similar, I believe, will play out with the systemic principles used in organizational constellations. They provide a potent tool for "seeing systems" without the cost or effort of assembling all the parts and players.[3] This book shows you how to look at an organization systemically, but it does not require you to use that approach overtly with a group. The challenge early adapters face is that the systemic process does not readily translate into the Newtonian language of business. The constellation methodology has not been around long enough to be the subject of scientific studies. This may change some day as the practice gains visibility. Till then, we can trust that the issue holders know if they obtained a useful insight or a practical solution.

You don't have to wait for some "authority" to validate this process.[3] Be your own scientist and experiment with this methodology to see if you find it helpful. Your personal experience is the terra firma to stand on. Just be sure to follow the guidelines in this book. Work with a skilled facilitator. Get proper training. Be ethical and use this approach where you have a mandate to facilitate change at levels that transcend cause and effect.

Perhaps in a few years the corporate shaman's systemic use of self and the tacit knowledge of the subconscious will hardly slant an eyebrow. In the meantime, if this book inspires people to look at and resolve business and professional issues more holistically it will be serving its purpose. For those early adapters, these words of Ralph Waldo Emerson are apt: *"Congratulate yourself if you have done something strange and extravagant and broken the monotony of a decorous age."* What was strange to Emerson's contemporaries is deemed weird in today's lexicon. If you want a creative and dynamic enterprise, however, then as the CEO of Zappos Tom Hseih said, *"a little weirdness is good."* The deep level of cognition this approach accesses will change your worldview. Enjoy the exploration. And, as you journey into terra incognita, don't forget this admonishment of the Dali Lama: *"Develop the heart/Too much energy in your country/Is spent developing the mind/Instead of the heart."*[4]

# Acknowledgments

Many people contributed to my development as a constellation facilitator and the learning experiences that enabled me to write this book. My thanks and gratitude are extended to all of them, including; Susan and John Ulfelder at the Hellinger Institute of Washington, DC, who conducted my initial training in family constellations, and Heinz Stark from Germany, who led the advanced training. Thanks to Jane Peterson in the United States; Ty Francis, Judith Hemming, and Barbara Morgan in the United Kingdom; Jan Jacob Stam of the Netherlands; and Cecillo Regojo from Portugal, who have all done much to advance systemic practices in the business world as well as generously provided their coaching and mentoring.

I am grateful for the connections Francesca Mason Boring, a Native-American constellation facilitator, has made between systemic work and traditional healing practices.

Fellow facilitators who have been active in my facilitator support group include Betsy Hostetler, Carol Heil, Mary Rentschler, Jim Shine, Beth Hand, Brenda Boyd, and Rani George. I much appreciate the dedication of Karen Porterfield, Katherine Krile, and Becca Archer (along with Brenda and Jim), who have all been mainstays of the Chesapeake Bay Organizational Development Network special interest group focused on systemic work.

Thanks to Rick Allen for his support in applying systemic concepts in the business world. Of course, all of us benefited from the visionary work of Bert Hellinger, the originator of family constellations, and Gunthard Weber, the father of organizational constellations.

Special thanks to constellation facilitators Jane Peterson and Jim Shine for their review of this manuscript and for their most helpful edits and suggestions. Special thanks also to my lovely wife, Stephanie, for her encouragement and editing; to Marlene Oulton, who provided the initial copyediting; and to Linda W. O'Doughda, for her professional editing of the final version of the manuscript. Thanks to Mark Weiman at Regent Press for his publishing expertise and patience with the revision process. And many thanks to Martha Mack and her team at Snow Mack Arts for their eye-catching front and back cover and chapter logo art. Finally, deepest gratitude for the blessings, guidance and personal growth I received from Bill Bauman and Thomas Hübl.

# Notes

## Overview

1. Myers-Briggs Type Indicator (MBTI) is the source code that most personality inventories are based on, and it is often used for team-building and self-awareness (http://en.wikipedia.org/wiki/Myers-Briggs Type Indicator). MBTI was developed in the 1940s by the mother-daughter team Katherine Cook Briggs and Isabel Briggs Myers. They based their "type indicator" on Carl Jung's groundbreaking book, *Psychological Types*, published in German in 1921. Jung's ideas about the nature of the human personality have not only endured nearly a hundred years, they have become more established and verified through numerous studies. Interestingly, he wrote the book to reconcile the contrasting therapeutic approaches of Freud (extroverted worldview) and Adler (introverted worldview). Visit http://en.wikipedia.org/wiki/Psychological Types for more information.

2. Appreciative Inquiry is a participative group problem-solving technique that focuses on what is working and what people take pride in. For more information, visit: http://www.centerforappreciativeinquiry.net/.

3. Open Space is a large group problem-solving activity that is fueled by empowerment and personal interest. Visit http://www.openspace-world.org/ for more details.

4. I became a teacher of Transcendental Meditation (TM) in the early 1970s. The founder of the practice realized the importance of scientific studies to demonstrate the benefits of meditating. In the early '80s, other teachers and I were teaching TM to business professionals in a number of countries.

5. Daniel Goleman drew upon the work of others, including a paper coauthored by John D. Mayer in 1990 on the concept of emotional intelligence. EQ is used in leadership development to enhance self-awareness. Visit http://www.danielgoleman.info/eq-in-the-workplace/.

## Introduction

1. See Daniel Goleman in note 2 for chapter 1.

2. James Fallows quotes Al Gore in "The Investment Secrets of Al Gore," *The Atlantic*, November 2015, 89.

3. http://climate.nasa.gov/scientific-consensus/. One reason why public opinion has not caught up with the overwhelming scientific consensus (97 percent of climate scientists) is the number of groups who actively deny there is a consensus.

4. http://win.niddk.nih.gov/statistics/. Nearly two out of three adults in the United States are overweight or obese according to an NIH study published in 2010.

5. I agree with the assertion but don't know the source for the 10-90 ratio. There is a widespread urban myth that we only use 10 percent of our mental capacity. If you equate capacity with brain activity far more of the brain is actually in use. Research shows that the subconscious plays a significant role in decision-making and problem-solving. Visit http://www.sciencedaily.com/releases/2013/02/130213092305.htm for more details.

6. Michael Lewis, *Moneyball: The Art of Winning an Unfair Game* (New York: W.W. Norton & Company, 2003). Lewis describes how the use of analysis and good conceptual thinking led to better decision-making for a major league baseball team.

7. M. Scott Peck, A World Waiting to Be Born: Civility Rediscovered (New York: Simon & Schuster, 1993), 13.

8. http://en.wikipedia.org/wiki/Campbell%27s_Law. The overreliance on data can end badly for more than a baseball team. Consider, for example, the number of primary and secondary schools that altered test scores to ensure that their students met NCLB performance standards. Donald Campbell's law states, "The more any quantitative social indicator (even some qualitative indicator) is used for social decision-making, the more subject it will be to corruption pressures and the more apt it will be to distort and corrupt the social processes it is intended to monitor." The old adage "Figures don't lie but liars figure" describes only half of what can go wrong. Keeping in mind the bigger picture, the overall context/purpose and guiding values has to be the other part of the decision-making process.

9. Alvin Toffler, *Future Shock* (New York: Bantam Books, 1970). It's a lame pun but true that Toffler was a futurist who was ahead of his time.

## Chapter 1

1. Jerry Harvey published the article "The Abilene Paradox: The Management of Agreement" in 1974. Harvey wrote how team members, opting not to "rock the boat," end up going along with a decision that in actually no one favors. https://en.wikipedia.org/wiki/Collective consciousness.

2. Robert Gass, *Chanting: Discovering Spirit in Sound* (New York: Broadway Books, 1999).

3. For more information about Peruvian Shamanism, see Bonnie Glass-Coffin and Oscar Miro-Quesada, *Lessons in Courage: Peruvian Shaman Wisdom for Everyday Life* (Faber, VA: Rainbow Ridge Books, 2014).

## Chapter 2

1. The myth of the Hero's Journey is one of the foundations of our worldview. For an updated discussion, Ken Davis offers some interesting thoughts in his article; see https://www.psychologytoday.com/blog/finding-love/201301/how-find-your-core-gifts-in-your-greatest-challenges.

2. www.thework.com. According to Byron Katie, if we change our "story" about our experiences we change our lives and choose to live with more joy and less pain.

3. http://en.wikipedia.org/wiki/K%C3%BCbler-Ross model.

4. Daniel Siegel, The Developing Mind: How Relationships and the Brain Interact to Shape Who We Are, 2nd edition (New York: Gilford Press, 2012).

5. Ibid., 5.

6. Steven Fogel, and Mark Rosin, Your Mind Is What Your Brain Does for a Living; Learn How to Make It Work for You (Austin, TX: Greenleaf Book Group Press, 2014). Fogel summarizes Siegel's work and applies the principles to his own personal development.

7. http://www.goodreads.com/author/quotes/312508.Virginia Satir.

8. This quote from Tennyson's letter comes from a source that somehow disappeared during one of the revisions of this book's manuscript. It will be included in a subsequent printing.

9. This exercise is based on a process led by Skip Ellis at a relationship workshop he conducted at his Institute for Integrated Self in Herndon, Virginia, in 2013.

10. Martin Buber, I and Thou, translated by Ronald Gregor Smith (New York: Charles Scribner's Sons, 1957). Buber is a dense read but rewarding. One reward is the insight gained in seeing the linkages between what he has to say and the many other exponents of self-development like Skip Ellis and Rose Rosetree. Strengthening your sense of self or "Thou" and managing it appropriately will enrich all your relationships.

11. I first heard the concept of the skilled empath in a workshop led by Rose Rosetree that I took in 2012. Fo r more information, see her book Becoming the Most Important Person in the Room: Your 30-Day Plan for Empath Empowerment (Sterling, VA: Woman's Intuition Worldwide, 2009).

12. These comments are gleaned from a presentation I attended led by Thomas Hübl in Washington, DC, in 2013 and his workshop in Jerusalem the following year. So many people try to avoid or suppress their feelings. Yet feelings connect the mind to the body and restore one's energy when experienced fully and released. See www. thomashuebl. com for more information on his teachings and workshops.

13. See http://mkp.org for more information on men's work. A related organization for women is Women Within at: http://womenwithin.org.

## Chapter 3

1. http://en.wikipedia.org/wiki/Systems_thinking.
2. See Peter Senge's explanation of system thinking that refers to a family at: http://www.mutualresponsibility.org/science/what-is-systems-thinking-peter-senge-explains-systems-thinking-approach-and-principles.
3. John Curtis Gowan, *Trance, Art, and Creativity: A Psychological Analysis of the Relationship between the Individual Ego and the Numinous Element in Three Modes: Prototaxic, Parataxic, and Syntaxic* (Scituate, MA: Creative Education Foundation, 1975).
4. Chip and Dan Heath, *Switch: How to Change Things When Change Is Hard* (New York: Broadway Books, 2010).
5. Ibid.
6. Stewart Wavell, Audrey Butt, and Nina Epton, *Trances* (Sydney: George Allen & Unwin Ltd., 1966).
7. Tom Roth, and Donald Clifton, *How Full Is Your Bucket? Positive Strategies for Work and Life* (Washington: Gallup Press, 2004). According to the authors, a positive atmosphere and the interactions that foster it leads to greater employee engagement.
8. http://www.goodreads.com/quotes/631583-a-mind-once-expanded-by-a-new-idea-never-returns.
9. Shri Nisargadatta Maharaj, *I Am That*, translated by Maurice Frydman (Bombay: Publisher Unknown, 1973).

## Chapter 4

1. I heard this "07 seconds" figure during a presentation by David Rock, but I have not been able to identify the actual source that Rock was quoting.
2. Andrew Blackman, "Inside the executive brain," the *Wall Street Journal,* April 28, 2014.
3. Lynne McTaggart, *The Field: The Quest for the Secret Forces in the Universe* (New York: HarperCollins, 2010), 22.
4. Ibid., 47.
5. Ibid., 121.
6. Ibid.
7. Karl Weick, *Social Psychology of Organizing* (Reading, MA: Addison Wesley, 1969).
8. McTaggart, *The Field*, 121.
9. http://science.nasa.gov/astrophysics/focus-areas/what-is-dark-energy/. One possibility, according to some researchers, is the existence of 10 to the order of 500 universes parallel to our own.
10. Michael Gerson, "A Golden Age of physics," the *Washington Post,* February 25, 2014, A30.
11. Bert Hellinger, *No Waves Without the Ocean: Experiences and Thoughts* (Heidelberg: Carl-Auer, 2006), 202.
12. Jonathan Merritt, "What every soul needs in a disintegrated world, the *Washington Post*, May 31, 2014, Religion: B2.

## Chapter 5

1. Francesca Mason Boring, *Connecting to Our Ancestral Past: Healing through Family Constellations, Ceremony, and Ritual* (Berkeley: North Atlantic Books, 2012), 50.
2. Rudolf Steiner, *Knowledge of Higher Worlds and Its Attainment* (New York: The Anthroposophic Press, 1947).
3. http://www.metaforum.com/en/pg-trainer/prof-matthias-varga-von-kibe3a9d-28germany29.html.
4. Bert Hellinger, *Loves Hidden Symmetry: What Makes Love Work in Relationships* (Phoenix: Zeig, Tucker & Co., 1998), 205.
5. Ibid., 206.
6. http://en.wikipedia.org/wiki/Johari_window. The self-awareness model known as the Johari Window was developed by Joe Luft and Harry Ingham in 1955. They combined their first names to give it a name. They reported later that an Indian colleague told them the word in Sanskrit meant the god who sees within.
7. One of those gifted coaches is Bill Bauman, who has been a mentor and coach to me for many years. For more information, visit http://www.billbauman.net.

## Chapter 6

1. Jakob Robert Schneider, *Family Constellations: Basic Principles and Procedures* (Heidelberg: Carl-Auer, 2007), 79. According to Schneider, Hellinger would quote Saint Augustine—"Love, and do what you like"—and then add, "And it's bound to be a disaster."
2. http://en.wikipedia.org/wiki/Enron and http://en.wikipedia.org/wiki/Enron scandal.
3. Bert Hellinger, *No Waves Without the Ocean: Experiences and Thoughts* (Heidelberg: Carl-Auer, 2006), 115.
4. M. Scott Peck, *A World Waiting to Be Born: Civility Rediscovered* (New York: Simon & Schuster, 1993), 38.
5. Schneider, *Family Constellations*, 37.
6. http://www.youtube.com/watch?v=3odvMJLGoCo is one of many YouTube videos of the monkey dance ritual that is used for community and social healing in Bali.
7. Francesca Mason Boring, *Connecting to Our Ancestral Past: Healing through Family Constellations, Ceremony, and Ritual* (Berkeley: North Atlantic Books, 2012), 14.

## Chapter 7

1. Malcolm Gladwell, *What the Dog Saw and Other Adventures* (Boston: Little Brown and Company, 2009).
2. Bert Hellinger, 2006, *No Waves Without the Ocean: Experiences and Thoughts*, (Heidelberg: Carl-Auer, 2006), 50. Hellinger believes that "Accusations hinder grief."
3. Bert Hellinger, *Success in Life: From the Series: Orders of Success*

(Berchtesgaden: Hellinger Publications, 2009), 66.

4. Jakob Robert Schneider, *Family Constellations: Basic Principles and Procedures* (Heidelberg: Carl-Auer, 2007), 75.

5. This adage came from Malidoma at a workshop he led in San Francisco in October 2012. His book *Of Water and the Spirit: Ritual, Magic and Initiation in the Life of an African Shaman* offers similar wisdom about the role of the ancestors according to the Dagara people in Burkina Faso.

6. Hellinger, *Success in Life,* 13.

7. Debra Mandel, *Your Boss Is Not Your Mother: Eight Steps to Eliminating Office Drama and Creating Positive Relationships at Work* (Evanston, IL: Agate Books, 2006).

8. Carl Jung, *Collected Works of C. G. Jung*, Vol. II (Princeton: Princeton University Press, 1973), 75.

9. M. Scott Peck, *A World Waiting to Be Born: Civility Rediscovered* (New York: Simon & Schuster, 1993), 10, 13.

10. According to Hellinger (in his *Love's Hidden Symmetry*, page 329), he was influenced by other researchers who explored this concept, including Ivan Boszormenyi-Nagy, who wrote *Invisible Bonds.*

11. The concept of current generations being affected by events in the lives of previous generations has been referred to in many books, including the Bible. In Exodus 34:7 (King James Version) we read: *". . .visiting the iniquity of the fathers upon the children, and upon the children's children, unto the third and to the fourth [generation]."*

## Chapter 8

1. This took place at a workshop Hellinger led in Washington, DC, in 2002 that I attended. He dismissed about four or five participants from the stage because they rambled on in response to his initial question concerning their desired outcome in working with him.

2. Bert Hellinger, *Loves Hidden Symmetry: What Makes Love Work in Relationships* (Phoenix: Zeig, Tucker & Co., 1998), 170.

3. This quote comes from a participant who attended a workshop led by Judith Hemming in Sidney, Australia, in 2013.

4. Bert Hellinger, *No Waves Without the Ocean: Experiences and Thoughts* (Heidelberg: Carl-Auer, 2006), 186–87.

5. Ibid., 244.

## Chapter 9

1. Visit www:strategicmodelbuilding.com/uploads/You_Inc_4_Player Model_Cards_2009.pdf for an outline of how the Four Player Model works.

2. http://en.wikipedia.org/wiki/Schr%C3%B6dinger%27s cat. Consider Erwin Schrödinger's famous quantum thought experiment with his hypothetical cat. Is Erwin's cat alive or dead? Both you and the cat won't know unless you open the box. Various realities are superimposed upon each other until your act of observation collapses the field of

possibilities, producing one reality (like a live cat) out of a multitude of possibilities. Schrödinger's thought experiment addresses the relationship of consciousness and the creation of personal reality in the context of quantum physics. What links Schrödinger's work to practical life is realizing the futility of searching for certainty in a world that is by design uncertain. In a quantum world the principle of superposition postulates that different realities exist at the same time. Introduce an observer, and those different realities collapse into the one the observer observes.

Another hypothesis is that the probability waves don't actually collapse to form the reality we observe. According to Max Tegmark's book *Our Mathematical Universe,* the waves branch off into parallel universes, which means we do as well.

3. http://www.goodreads.com/quotes/search?utf8=%E2%9C%93&q=virginia+satir.

4. Ulrich Dupree, *Ho'oponopono: The Hawaiian Forgiveness Ritual as the Key to Your Life's Fulfillment* (Forres, Scotland: Findhorn Press, 2012). The four tenets for creating peace and healing are these: I am sorry, please forgive me, I love you, and thank you. You use these tenets to "treat" yourself because the other person's problem or offense also exists within you.

## Part II title page
1. Malcolm Gladwell, *What the Dog Saw and Other Adventures* (Boston: Little Brown and Company, 2009), 153.

## Chapter 10
1. For more information on "the theory that explains everything," see http://www.spiraldynamics.net/.

## Chapter 11
1. Bert Hellinger, *Loves Hidden Symmetry: What Makes Love Work in Relationships* (Phoenix: Zeig, Tucker & Co., 1998), 92. The role of parents is to give and that of children to take. It is inherently an unequal relationship with an important distinction. *"Love succeeds when children value the life they have been given—when they take their parents as parents as they are."*

2. http://www.goodreads.com/quotes/search?commSearch&page=5&q=joseph+campbell+&utf8=%E2%9C%93.

3. Lawrence R. Samuel, *Freud on Madison Avenue: Motivation Research and Subliminal Advertising in America* (Philadelphia: Penn Press, 2013).

## Chapter 12
1. The term "management constellation" was coined by constellation facilitators Katharina Lingg, Claude Rosselet, and Georg Senoner. It

refers to helping a business team collectively reflect on a specific task or question related to the purpose of the team.

2. Robert W. Jacobs, and Kathleen D. Dannemiller, *Real-Time Strategic Change* (San Francisco: Berrett-Koehler Publishers,1994).

3. Jakob Robert Schneider, *Family Constellations: Basic Principles and Procedures* (Heidelberg: Carl-Auer, 2007), 143.

4. For more information on this innovative corporate structure that bills itself as management without management, visit http://holacracy.org/.

## Chapter 13

1. Presentation on Adult Development by Penny Potter at the Chesapeake Bay Organizational Development Network in 2015. Assessments developed by Lectica Corporation look at the capacity for systems thinking to measure leadership ability. The ability to grasp the complexity of multiple systems is the trademark of elite leaders who represent a small fraction of the population.

2. Robert McCartney, "Until Metro officials take safety seriously, delay could be measured in deaths," the *Washington Post*, February 25, 2010, B1.

3. Ann Scott Tyson, "Metro's downhill slide: No clear answers on transit agency's safety, budget woes," the *Washington Post*, February 21, 2010, A1.

4. Lena Sun, and Joe Stephens, "Scathing federal report dissects safety at Metro; Investigators fault transit agency leaders, monitoring committee," the *Washington Post*, March 5, 2010, A1, A15.

5. http://www.wmata.com/about_metro/general_manager/index2.cfm.

6. http://www.washingtonpost.com/local/trafficandcommuting/oneddead-two-injured-in-metro-tunnel-explosion/2013/10/06/88ae94a8-2c6111e3-8ade-a1f23cda135e_story.html.

7. http://www.washingtonpost.com/local/metro-wins-gold-award-for-safety-5-years-after-red-line-crash-but-hard-tasks-still-remain/2014/06/21/28042796-f8e2-11e3-a606-946fd632f9f1_story.html.

8. Julie Zauzmer, "A place to honor Metro crash victims," the *Washington Post*, June 23, 2014, B1.

9. The Metro saga continues according to media stories about the subway system's mishaps in both operations and administration. Check out this story in the *Washington Post* at: http://www.washingtonpost.com/local/trafficandcomming/2015/06/06/ad5806b6-0a24-11e5-a7ad-b430fc1d3f5c_story.html.

## Chapter 14

1. Being an honest broker is unlikely when you consciously favor one side over the other. It is even more unlikely when that bias is unconscious. Peacemaking activities at Neve Shalom show the depth of complexity to be addressed. For more information, see: Grace Feuerverger, *Oasis of Dreams: Teaching and Learning Peace in a Jewish-Palestinian Village*

*in Israel* (Falmer, NY: Routledge, 2001). To learn about Neve Shalom, which was founded by Wellesley Aron, visit http://wasns.org/.

2. Comments by the participants after the workshop included: "It was a very powerful experience and I'm glad I had the opportunity to witness as a participant and observer. My spirit certainly felt lighter on the drive home" and "I appreciated the opportunity to become more aware of my unconscious self. During the original exercise at the beginning of class, we were able to experience this new form of human connection."

## Chapter 15

1. Virginia Satir, *The New Peoplemaking* (Palo Alto: Science and Behavior Books, 1988).
2. http://www.goodreads.com/author/quotes/20105.Joseph_Campbell. The full quote is, "Follow your bliss and the universe will open doors for you where there were only walls."
3. Joseph Campbell, *The Hero with a Thousand Faces,* 3rd edition (Novata, CA: New World Library, 2008).
4. I am not sure who the source of the saying is who suggests that the parts of yourself you reject will turn against you. It sounds like something Joseph Campbell or Robert Bly or Carl Jung would say — to name just a few.

## Chapter 16

1. http://www.washingtonpost.com/national/health-science/study-finds-that-fear-can-travel-quickly-through-generations-of-mice-dna/2013/12/07/94dc97f2-5e8e-11e3-bc56-c6ca94801fac_story.html. This study deals with mice. There are others that show similar tendencies in humans. Interestingly, positive traits and circumstances also show up in previous generations, so these phenomena work both ways.
2. Daniel Siegel, *The Developing Mind: How Relationships and the Brain Interact to Shape Who We Are,* 2nd edition (New York: Gilford Press, 2012).
3. Bert Hellinger, *Success in Life: From the Series: Orders of Success* (Berchtesgaden: Hellinger Publications, 2009), 13.
4. Scott Stossel, "Thanks, Mom: Revisiting the Famous Harvard Study of What Makes People Truly Successful," *The Atlantic,* May 2013, 22. If you are wondering why there were no women in the study it's because when the study began in 1938 Harvard did not enroll female students. Another interesting finding was that warm childhood relationships with fathers correlated with great life satisfaction at age seventy-five, whereas the relationship with the mother did not make a difference.
5. Ibid., 22.

## Chapter 17

1. Tom Huber, manager of the Dividend Growth Fund, quoted in the article "A Renewed Rise in M&A: Is It Good for Investors," *T. Rowe Price Report,* Issue No. 125, Fall 2014, 6.

## Chapter 18

1. Aldous Huxley, *The Perennial Philosophy: An Interpretation of the Great Mystics, East and West* (New York: HarperCollins, 1945).
2. Action Learning refers both to experiential team-building activities and to a team-based problem-solving model. For the first reference, visit http://ebtd.aee.org/ebtd; for the second reference, see Michael Marquardt, *Optimizing the Power of Action Learning: Real-Time Strategies for Developing Leaders, Building Teams and Transforming Organizations* (Boston: Nicholas Brealey, 2011).
3. EQi is a test of emotional intelligence applying the concepts of Dr. Reuven Bar-On .
4. Situational Leadership provides a template for how managers should manage employees who are at different levels of development. For more information, visit http://en.wikipedia.org/wiki/Situational_leadership_theory.

## Chapter 19

1. http://www.goodreads.com/quotes/search?utf8=%E2%9C%93&q=virginia+satir& commit=Search.

## Chapter 20

1. http://www.goodreads.com/author/quotes/5255891.Steve_Jobs?page=5. The actual quote from Good Reads is: *"Some people say, 'Give the customers what they want.' But that's not my approach. Our job is to figure out what they're going to want before they do. I think Henry Ford once said, 'If I'd asked customers what they wanted, they would have told me, "A faster horse!"'* People don't know what they want until you show it to them. That's why I never rely on market research. Our task is to read things that are not yet on the page."
2. Harrison Snow, *The Power of Team-Building Using Ropes Techniques* (San Diego, CA: Pfeiffer & Company, 1993).
3. For an excellent book about seeing systems—the top, middle, and bottom parts—see Berry Oshry, *Seeing Systems: Unlocking the Mysteries of Organizational Life* (San Francisco: Berrett-Koehler, 2007).
4. http://www.goodreads.com/author/quotes/570218.Dalai_Lama_XIV?page=2.

# Literature

Berne, Eric. *What Do You Say After You Say Hello? The Psychology of Human Destiny.* London: Random House, 1975.

Boring, Francesca Mason. *Connecting to Our Ancestral Past: Healing through Family Constellations, Ceremony, and Ritual.* Berkeley: North Atlantic Books, 2012.

Buber, Martin. *I and Thou.* Translated by Ronald Gregor Smith. New York: Charles Scribner's Sons, 1957.

Fogel, Steven, and Mark Rosin. *Your Mind Is What Your Brain Does for a Living: Learn How to Make It Work for You.* Austin, TX: Greenleaf Book Group Press, 2014.

Gass, Robert. *Chanting: Discovering Spirit in Sound.* New York: Broadway, 1999.

Glass-Coffin, Bonnie, and Oscar Miro-Quesada. *Lessons in Courage: Peruvian Shaman Wisdom for Everyday Life.* Faber, VA: Rainbow Ridge, 2014.

Gowan, John Curtis. *Trance, Art, and Creativity: A Psychological Analysis of the Relationship between the Individual Ego and the Numinous Element in Three Modes: Prototaxic, Parataxic, and Syntaxic.* Scituate, MA: Creative Education Foundation, 1975.

Harner, Michael. *The Way of the Shaman.* San Francisco: Harper Collins, 1990.

Hellinger, Bert. *Loves Hidden Symmetry: What Makes Love Work in Relationships.* Phoenix: Zeig, Tucker & Co., 1998.

Hellinger, Bert. *No Waves Without the Ocean: Experiences and Thoughts.* Heidelberg: Carl-Auer, 2006.

Hellinger, Bert. *Success in Life: From the Series: Orders of*

*Success.* Berchtesgaden: Hellinger Publications, 2009.

Horn, Klaus P., and Regine Brick. *Invisible Dynamics: Systemic Constellations in Organizations and in Business.* Heidelberg: Carl-Auer, 2005.

Jacobs, Robert W., and Kathleen Dannemiller. *Real-Time Strategic Change.* San Francisco: Berrett-Koehler Publishers, 1994.

Königswieser, Roswita, and Martin Hillebrand. *Systemic Consultancy in Organisations: Concepts, Tools, Innovations.* Heidelberg: Carl-Auer, 2005.

Lewis, Michael. *Moneyball: The Art of Winning an Unfair Game.* New York: W.W. Norton & Company, 2003.

Maharaj, Shri Nisargadatta. *I Am That.* Translated by Maurice Frydman. Bombay,1973.

Mandel, Debra. *Your Boss Is Not Your Mother: Eight Steps to Eliminating Office Drama and Creating Positive Relationships at Work.* Evanston, IL: Agate Books, 2006.

Marquardt, Michael. *Optimizing the Power of Action Learning: Real-time Strategies for Developing Leaders, Building Teams and Transforming Organizations.* Boston: Nicholas Brealey, 2011.

McTaggart, Lynne. *The Field: The Quest for the Secret Forces in the Universe.* New York: HarperCollins, 2010.

Peck, M. Scott. *The Different Drum: Community Making and Peace.* New York: Simon & Schuster, 1984.

Peck, M. Scott. *A World Waiting to Be Born: Civility Rediscovered.* New York: Simon & Schuster, 1993.

Ortberg, John. *Soul Keeping: Caring for the Most Important Part of You.* Grand Rapids, MI: Zondervan, 2014.

Rosetree, Rose. *Becoming the Most Important Person in the Room: Your 30-Day Plan for Empath Empowerment.* Sterling, VA: Woman's Intuition Worldwide, 2009.

Schneider, Jakob Robert. *Family Constellations: Basic Principles and Procedures.* Heidelberg: Carl-Auer, 2007.

Siegel, Daniel. *The Developing Mind: How Relationships and the Brain Interact to Shape Who We Are.* New York: The Guilford Press, 1999.

Simon, Fritz B., Author Group of *C/O/N/E/C/T/A. The Organization of the Self-Organization: Foundations of Systemic Management.* Carl-Auer, Heidelberg, 2004.

Somé, Malidoma Patrice. *Of Water and the Spirit: Ritual, Magic and Initiation in the Life of an African Shaman.* New York: Penguin Group, 1994.

Toffler, Alvin. *Future Shock.* New York: Bantam Books, 1970.

Tzu, Lao. *Tao Te Ching.* Translated by Jonathan Star. New York: Penguin, 2008.

Weick, K. *Social Psychology of Organizing.* Reading, PA: Addison-Wesley, 1969.

Wilber, Ken. *The Essential Ken Wilber: An Introductory Reader.* Boston: Shambhala Publications, 1998.

# About the Author

As the Director of Team Building Associates since 1988, Harrison Snow has been helping government and corporate clients in twenty-six different countries manage change and enhance organizational performance. His expertise is in the areas of change management, strategic planning, leadership training, executive coaching, and team-building facilitation. Harrison helps managers and their teams define and discuss sensitive issues, gain new insights, reach useful agreements, and implement key actions that improve engagement and performance. He also conducts train-the-facilitator programs to develop the skills of professional facilitators. His clients include the World Bank, International Finance Corporation, Inter-American Development Bank, U.S. Agency for International Development, and the U.S. Department of State as well as a number of Fortune 500 companies. Over the years, Harrison has facilitated programs for nearly a hundred organizations and thousands of participants. He resides in the Washington, DC, metro area with his wife and son. For more information on the programs and workshops he offers, visit: http://teambuildingassociates.com.

CPSIA information can be obtained
at www.ICGtesting.com
Printed in the USA
BVOW03s2153141116
467852BV00012B/118/P